THE DOS BOOK

ELECTRONIC LEARNING FACILITATORS, INC.

HARCOURT BRACE JOVANOVICH, PUBLISHERS
San Diego   New York   Chicago   Austin   Washington, D.C.
London   Sydney   Tokyo   Toronto

WordPerfect is a trademark of WordPerfect Corporation. Lotus 1-2-3 and Symphony are trademarks of Lotus Development Corporation. dBASE III Plus and Multimate are trademarks of Ashton-Tate. MS-DOS, Multiplan, and Microsoft Word are trademarks of Microsoft Corporation. VP-planner is a trademark of Paperback Software. SuperCalc3 is a trademark of Computer Associates International. IBM PC, IBM XT, IBM PC/AT, and PC-DOS are trademarks of International Business Machines Corporation. WordStar, MailMerge, and SpellStar are trademarks of MicroPro International Corporation.

Copyright © 1989 by Harcourt Brace Jovanovich, Inc.

All rights reserved. No part of this publication may be reproduced or transmitted in any form or by any means, electronic or mechanical, including photocopy, recording, or any information storage and retrieval system, without permission in writing from the publisher.

Requests for permission to make copies of any part of the work should be mailed to: Permissions, Harcourt Brace Jovanovich, Publishers, Orlando, Florida 32887.

ISBN: 0-15-517921-7

Library of Congress Catalog Card Number: 88-83504

Printed in the United States of America

INTRODUCTION

Course Objectives

This course is designed to prepare students to use IBM and IBM-compatible computers in a business environment. An understanding of basic computer concepts in general and of the operating system in particular will enable students to more easily understand and learn the specific application programs they will encounter. All participants will:

- Gain familiarity with basic terminology, concepts, and functions of microcomputers

- Understand the purpose, capabilities, and limitations of an operating system in general and IBM DOS in particular

- Discuss and use all the fundamental DOS commands, appreciating DOS's importance in file, disk, and hardware management

- Understand the physical and logical organization of hard disks

- Be able to format a bootable hard disk and design and manage a hard disk directory structure

- Use the EDLIN editor and COPY command to create DOS files

- Understand batch programming and create and use batch files, including AUTOEXEC.BAT, for automating tasks and customizing systems

- Create a menu system for automating DOS control

- Explore system setup and installation of application packages

Guide to the Use of the Manual

The following conventions have been used in this manual:

- All commands, words, and phrases to be entered by the user are typed in CAPITAL letters. You may enter DOS commands in upper- or lowercase letters.

- Press the [Return] (Enter) key after each DOS command or line of text to be entered. You will not be instructed to do so in the manual.

- Keys to be pressed are specified in square brackets []; for example, the Escape key is written [Esc]; the F6 key as [F6].

- Keys to be pressed simultaneously will be shown together, as [Ctrl][Scroll Lock].

- All Activities are presented in a two-column format:

    the left column describes the <u>Task</u> to be done

    the right column details the <u>Procedure</u> (actual commands to enter) to perform the task

- You will receive a student disk containing the following files:

    READ.ME
    FREE.COM
    FREE.DOC
    SDIR.COM
    SDIR.DOC
    LIST.COM
    MEMO.TXT
    WORDS.TXT
    HELLO1.TXT
    NOTICE

- You will need an extra formatted floppy disk for ACTIVITY 9-3.

System Setup

Because this course is designed to prepare students to work with IBM and IBM-compatible computers in a business environment, a great deal of emphasis is placed on those aspects of DOS that relate to the use of a computer with a hard disk on which multiple programs and data files are stored—the configuration most popular in the workplace today.

The activities presented here assume a <u>minimum</u> system configuration for each workstation as follows:

- An IBM or IBM-compatible computer with at least 256 Kb RAM

- DOS version 3.0 or higher

- One 10-megabyte or larger hard disk, designated as drive C:

- One floppy disk drive, designated as drive A:

- Organization of drive C: into subdirectories, with DOS external programs either in the root directory or, preferably, in a subdirectory named \DOS or \UTIL or another name in standard acceptance

    An AUTOEXEC.BAT file with the following lines:
      DATE
      TIME
      PATH C:\;C:\DOS name of directory storing DOS programs

    Application programs, in their own subdirectories, available on the hard disk (a popular word processor, database manager and spreadsheet are used as examples here; students should be informed of the programs available on their hard disk)

    Access by each workstation to a printer

    A color monitor is necessary for ACTIVITY 9-2; if a color monitor is not available, this ACTIVITY could be discussed but not carried out

<u>Dual Floppy System</u>: Where appropriate, individual activities have been redesigned for a two-floppy system (drives A: and B:). These activities for UNIT III are in APPENDIX A; the UNIT IV activity is in APPENDIX B. With dual floppies, it is assumed that a bootable DOS disk is available for each computer's A: drive; the student disk will be inserted into drive B: The AUTOEXEC.BAT file on the DOS disk should contain a PATH A:\ statement, with all the DOS external commands available on the disk.

TABLE OF CONTENTS

Introduction

UNIT I: Introduction to Microcomputer Hardware and Software 1
    Computer Hardware 2
    Computer Memory 3
    Input/Output Devices 3
    Computer Software 8
    Microfloppies 9
    Rules for Floppy Disk Care 9
    SUMMARY 11
    QUICK CHECK 12

UNIT II: Identifying the Role of Personal Computers in
       the Workplace 13
    Word Processing 14
    Desktop Publishing 15
    Database Management Systems 16
    Spreadsheets 19
    Graphics 21
    Communications 21
    Networking 23
    SUMMARY 24
    QUICK CHECK 25

UNIT III: Introduction to the DOS Operating System 27
    Operating Systems 28
    DOS and Beyond 29
    DOS Filename Rules 30
    DOS Global Filename Characters 32
    Fundamental DOS Commands 33
    Internal Commands 33
    External Commands 34
    Command Options 34
    Controlling DOS 35
    "Booting Up" 36
    ACTIVITY 3-1: Getting Started 37
    ACTIVITY 3-2: DOS Housekeeping Commands 39
    ACTIVITY 3-3: Displaying a Disk's Contents 41
    ON YOUR OWN 43
    The COPY Command 44
    ACTIVITY 3-4: Copying and Verifying Files 45
    DISKCOPY and DISKCOMP 47

ACTIVITY 3-5: Deleting Files 48
ACTIVITY 3-6: Viewing the Contents of a File 49
Redirecting Input and Output 50
ACTIVITY 3-7: Redirecting Output 51
Using Pipes and Filters 52
ACTIVITY 3-8: Variations on Type 53
ON YOUR OWN 55
SUMMARY 57
QUICK CHECK 59

UNIT IV: Additional External Commands 61
    The PRINT Command 62
    ACTIVITY 4-1: PRINT 63
    The RECOVER Command 64
    The ATTRIB Command 65
    ACTIVITY 4-2: ATTRIB 66
    The CHKDSK Command 67
    ACTIVITY 4-3: Checking Disk Validity 69
    The ASSIGN Command 71
    The MODE Command 72
    ACTIVITY 4-4: MODE 74
    ON YOUR OWN 76
    SUMMARY 78
    QUICK CHECK 79

UNIT V: Disk Organization 81
    The FORMAT Command 83
    Physical Organization 84
    Hard Disk Organization 85
    Formatting and Maintaining a Hard Disk 86
    Logical Organization: Tree-Structured Directory 86
    Guidelines for Creating Subdirectories 87
    DOS Subdirectory Commands 88
    Moving Between Directories 89
    ACTIVITY 5-1: Navigating a Tree-Structured Directory 90
    ACTIVITY 5-2: Simulating a Hard Disk 91
    ACTIVITY 5-3: Creating a Tree-Structured Directory 93
    The PROMPT Command 96
    ACTIVITY 5-4: Creating Customized Prompts 97
    ACTIVITY 5-5: Completing the Tree-Structured Directory .. 98
    File Specification 100
    ACTIVITY 5-6: Copying Files into a Subdirectory 101
    The PATH Command 104
    ACTIVITY 5-7: Setting and Using Paths 105
    The SUBST Command 106

ON YOUR OWN	107
SUMMARY	108
QUICK CHECK	109

UNIT VI: Creating DOS Files ... 111
The COPY Command Revisited	112
ACTIVITY 6-1: Using COPY to Create a DOS File	113
File Creation and Editing Using EDLIN	114
Use of Function Keys and Editing Keys with EDLIN	115
ACTIVITY 6-2: Using EDLIN to Edit HELLO.TXT	116
ACTIVITY 6-3: Creating a File with EDLIN	118
ON YOUR OWN	119
SUMMARY	120
QUICK CHECK	121

UNIT VII: Batch Files ... 123
Batch Files	124
Similarities/Differences between Batch Files and Text Files	125
ACTIVITY 7-1: Creating a Batch File to Display the Contents of a File and Change Directories	126
ACTIVITY 7-2: Creating a Simple Batch File to Prevent Accidental Formatting of a Hard Disk	129
Batch File Variables	131
Exiting from a Batch File	131
ACTIVITY 7-3: Creating a More Sophisticated Batch File to Prevent Accidental Formatting of a Hard Disk	133
AUTOEXEC.BAT	137
ACTIVITY 7-4: Creating and Using an AUTOEXEC.BAT File	138
ON YOUR OWN	139
SUMMARY	140
QUICK CHECK	141

UNIT VIII: Creating a Menu System ... 143
Command and Menu-Driven Systems	145
Menu Characteristics	146
Steps in Menu Creation	147
Mapping a Directory (Tree) Structure	148
Using Extended-Character Set Graphics	150
ACTIVITY 8-1: Creating the Menu Text File	151
ACTIVITY 8-2: Creating the Batch File that Calls MENU.TXT	152

　　　　ACTIVITY 8-3: Creating Batch Files to Change
　　　　　　Directories and Load Applications 153
　　　　ACTIVITY 8-3: For Systems without Available
　　　　　　Application Programs 155
　　　　ACTIVITY 8-4: Automating the Menu System 157
　　　　SUMMARY 158
　　　　QUICK CHECK 159

UNIT IX: System Management 161
　　　　Installing Applications 162
　　　　Configuring Your System 163
　　　　Creating a Virtual Disk 165
　　　　Configuring Your Screen and Keyboard with ANSI.SYS 166
　　　　Altering the Monitor Display 167
　　　　Using ANSI.SYS to Position the Cursor 168
　　　　Redefining Keyboard Keys 168
　　　　ACTIVITY 9-1: Creating a CONFIG.SYS File 169
　　　　ACTIVITY 9-2: Using ANSI.SYS commands 170
　　　　Backing Up a Hard Disk 171
　　　　ACTIVITY 9-3: Backing Up Selected Files from the
　　　　　　Hard Disk to a Floppy Disk 172
　　　　ON YOUR OWN 173
　　　　SUMMARY 174
　　　　QUICK CHECK 175

APPENDIX A: Activities from UNIT III for Dual Floppy
　　　Systems　　.. 177

APPENDIX B: Activities from UNIT IV for Dual Floppy
　　　Systems　　.. 197

APPENDIX C: Answers to Quick Checks and On Your Own 199

Index 212

UNIT·1·

Introduction to Microcomputer Hardware and Software

Overview: Personal computers are rapidly changing the organization, processing and analysis of information in the workplace. The personal computer provides the user with a powerful information processing system. To appreciate and apply this power, it is essential that the user have a basic understanding of how computers function, of the vital relationship between hardware and software, and of the terminology of this exciting field.

Topics: Computer Hardware

Computer Memory

Input/Output Devices

Computer Software

Computer Hardware

Computer systems are made up of a number of component parts; none of these parts can stand alone. The main component, the central processing unit (CPU), depends on adequate memory and assorted peripherals to become a functional computing system.

The CPU is referred to as the "brain" of the computer system. It is the large-scale integrated chip located on the motherboard of all personal computers. The IBM PC uses an Intel 8088 chip; newer, faster, and more powerful computers use the 80286 chip (IBM AT and compatible computers) or the 80386 chip (some IBM PS/2 computers and other manufacturers' "386" machines). Every action taken by the computer is directly or indirectly controlled by the CPU.

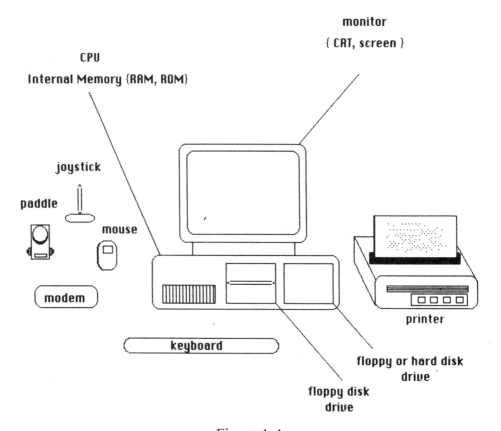

Figure 1-1

Computer Memory

Computer memory exists as ROM, read-only memory, and RAM, random-access memory. ROM contains programs that control the basic functioning of the computer; the user does not alter the contents of ROM. RAM is the memory available to the user for applications and programming. Programs and data in RAM are erased whenever the computer power is turned off. Computer memory is measured in kilobytes, K, (1024 bytes). A byte is the amount of memory required to store one character; therefore, a computer with a memory of 256K can store 256 * 1024 or 267,144 characters.

Input/Output (I/O) Devices

One of the most powerful abilities of the computer is that of communicating with the outside world through peripheral devices such as monitors, keyboards, printers, and modems. Together the peripherals are called "I/O devices" which stands for "Input/Output" because they allow information to be entered into and sent from the computer.

Keyboards, paddles, mice, and joysticks are all input devices. They are the primary way that information is entered into the computer's memory. Keyboard layout and keys differ among various IBM PC models. The original IBM PC keyboard (Figure 1-4) has the function keys to the left of the keyboard, while the new PS/2 line of computers has the function keys across the top of the keyboard (Figure 1-5). Additionally the PS/2 line has separate cursor control keys and lighted Num Lock, Caps Lock, and Scroll Lock indicators. Monitors and printers are the main output devices. Monitors come in monochrome or full color and differ from home television sets in their vastly superior resolution. Printers can be letterquality, dot matrix, ink jet, thermal, or laser. Each produces a slightly different quality print at varying speed and cost. Disk drives and modems are classified as dual I/O devices because they both input information into the computer and store output from the computer. Disk drives store and retrieve commercial and user-developed programs on floppy disks. (See SOFTWARE.) Modems allow computers to talk to each other via the telephone lines and access data from distant on-line data bases.

All peripheral devices are connected to the controlling board, the motherboard, inside the chassis of the computer. Each device—the monitor, the keyboard, the printers, the diskdrives, etc.—plugs into an outlet, or port, either on the motherboard itself or on another board, or expansion card, which in turn plugs into a slot on the motherboard.

4   The DOS Book

Inside the IBM XT

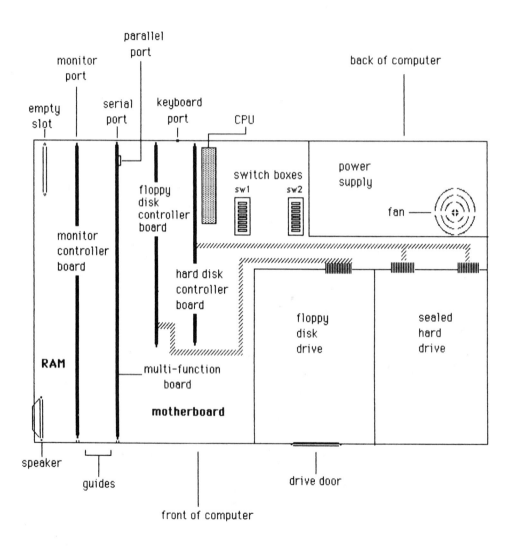

Figure 1-2

Unit I 5

IBM KEYBOARD

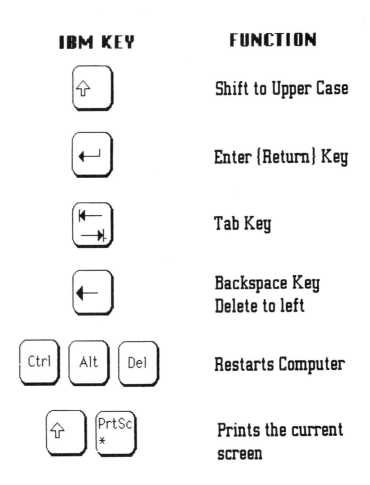

Figure 1-3

6 The DOS Book

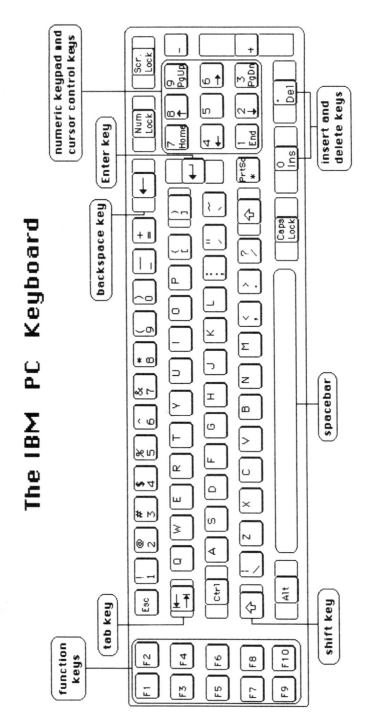

Figure 1-4

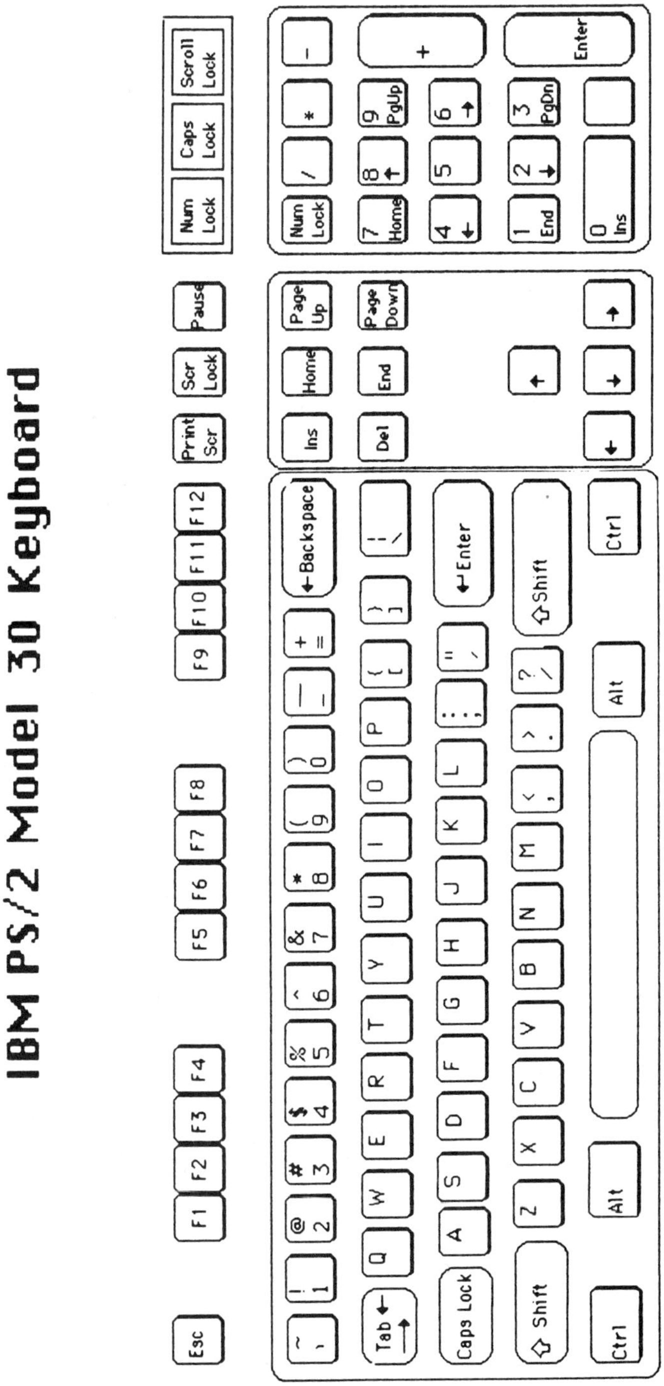

Unit I 7

IBM PS/2 Model 30 Keyboard

Figure 1-5

Information Flow within a Microcomputer System

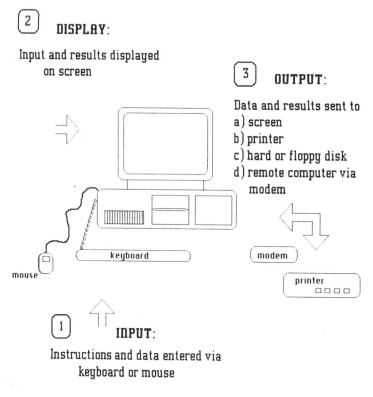

Figure 1-6

Computer Software

Software is the collective name for the various computer programs. A program is a set of detailed step-by-step instructions that provides the computer all the information it will need to communicate with its peripheral devices and perform a variety of tasks. When purchasing software, it is important to ascertain whether it will run under your computer's operating system and be compatible with additional expansion cards that have been installed in your computer. An operating system is a collection of programs that is automatically loaded into memory when the computer is turned on. The operating system enables the computer to communicate with its peripherals. IBM and compatible computers run under the DOS operating system.

In 1988 IBM began selling a new operating system for use with 80286- and 80386-chip computers. This operating system, called OS/2, permits multitasking—using the computer for several (up to 16!) different functions simultaneously. The user can easily switch the screen to view the current status of each program as all the programs continue processing. Each program runs under OS/2 as if it were operating on a separate computer—a database program can be sorting a large file, a communications program can be requesting information from another computer, and the user can be composing a memo on a word-processing program—all safely and efficiently. Many software programs that were written to be used with DOS will also run under OS/2. New programs are being written to take advantage of the enhanced capabilities of OS/2.

Software is stored on floppy and hard disks. The IBM PC uses the standard 5 1/4" double-sided, double density floppy disk, which can store about 360,000 characters of data; the IBM XT and AT have both a floppy disk drive and a 20 megabyte (20 million characters of storage) or larger hard disk. AT computers may have a "high density" disk drive in addition to a standard double-density disk drive. High-density floppy disks can store about 720,000 bytes. Hard disks are sealed into the computer or in a stand-alone unit, and are never handled by the user. Floppy disks are permanently encased in a plastic jacket, but require care in use.

Microfloppies

The latest additions to the IBM family of computers, the PS/2 models, have a 3 1/2" microfloppy drive as well as a hard disk. The microfloppies can easily be carried in a shirt pocket and are encased in a hard plastic surface that does not expose the read/write area of the disk until it is inside the disk drive. The 3 1/2" disk requires no protective sleeve and is less susceptible to damage than the 5 1/4" floppy. These new disks can store about 1.4 million characters.

Rules For Floppy Disk Care

The following basic rules must be observed when handling 5 1/4" floppy disks:

- Never touch the exposed surface that is visible through the oval window of the jacket.

- Keep the disk in its protective sleeve.

- Magnetic fields such as those produced by a ringing telephone or television can destroy data on your disk.

- "Floppy" refers to the disk's flexible nature, not your option to bend, fold, or mutilate.

- Use a felt-tipped pen to write on disk labels; or better still, write on the label before putting it on the disk.

Summary—Introduction to Microcomputer Hardware and Software

1. The main parts of a microcomputer system are hardware, software, and peripheral input/output devices. No single part of the system is of any use without the other parts.

2. Computer hardware consists of the CPU or central processing unit—the chip that is the "brain" of the computer—and memory, both ROM and RAM.

3. I/O devices provide the means for data to get into the computer's memory and to be sent from the computer so that the user can see results of processing.

4. Software consists of computer programs, instructions that tell the computer how to perform various functions.

5. A major type of software is an operating system, the instructions that tell the computer how to communicate with the other parts of the system and that allow user control over the system.

6. Software is stored on floppy and hard disks. These media will contain the data the user creates and manipulates with the computer; they should be treated with care to safeguard that data.

12 The DOS Book

Quick Check—Introduction to Microcomputer Hardware and Software

1. The three main parts of a microcomputer system are:
    a. Cables
    b. I/O devices
    c. RAM
    d. Software
    e. Hardware
    f. ROM
    g. Chips

2. What kind of devices are the keyboard, mouse, joystick?
    a. Remote communications
    b. Storage
    c. Input
    d. Output

3. What kind of devices are monitors and printers?
    a. Remote communications
    b. Storage
    c. Input
    d. Output

4. Floppy disks, microfloppies, and hard disks are forms of
    a. permanent storage.
    b. random access memory (RAM).
    c. read only memory (ROM).
    d. application programs.

5. An operating system (circle all correct answers)
    a. enables the computer to communicate with all parts of the system.
    b. must be loaded into memory each time the computer is turned on.
    c. can work with all application programs.
    d. is permanently stored on a floppy or hard disk.
    e. can allow the computer to do more than one task at a time.
    f. is used to sort large database files.

UNIT·2·

Identifying the Role of Personal Computers in the Workplace

Overview: Computers have a wide array of capabilities. This section will explore the major uses for personal computers for business and personal use.

Topics: Word Processing

Desktop Publishing

Database Management Systems

Spreadsheets

Graphics

Communications

Networking

Word Processing

Word-processing software makes up a large part of all software sold. The art of writing has been revolutionized by the advent of relatively inexpensive computer systems. It is this cost reduction that has brought the power of word processing into the hands of the general population. The number of people using computers for word processing is projected to increase dramatically in the next five years.

Word processing is powerful because it allows the author to make almost any changes required in a matter of seconds. If a paragraph is added or deleted, the word processing software automatically reformats the document to accommodate the change. Characters, words, and sentences can be inserted and deleted at will. The edited document is saved to a floppy or hard disk and can be sent to a printer for "hard copy." In addition, considerable flexibility exists for printing out the final copy. Options for boldface, underlining, and altering margins are a part of all word-processing software.

Desktop Publishing

Desktop publishing is rapidly becoming a very popular extension of word processing. Desktop publishing programs can "import" text created by a word processor and add charts or pictures created by a graphics program. These programs allow the user to define different typestyles and sizes (for example, large fancy type for headlines, italics for book titles), as well as column widths and picture placement. When used in combination with a laser printer, desktop publishing programs can produce output which rivals professional typesetting.

Word Processing Software
in the Workplace

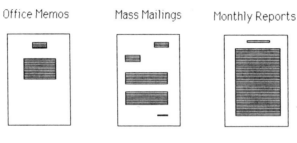

Office Memos   Mass Mailings   Monthly Reports

You can throw out:
    Carbon paper   White-out
    Scissors   Correcting tape
    Scotch tape   Stacks of paper

You will be able to:
    Edit documents on screen
    Cut and paste on screen
    Format the printed page by setting
      margins, tabs, line spacing
    Use **bold**, <u>underline</u>, *italics*, _{small print}
    Check the spelling of documents
    Merge addresses with base letters

Figure 2-1

Database Management Systems

Database management programs allow the user to computerize record systems that have previously been manipulated by hand. Virtually any type of filing system or list can be computerized with such software. Once the form or structure of the database has been determined and the data entered, the user can rearrange (sort), query, and print the database in an infinite variety of configurations. Many database programs have built-in mathematical and statistical functions in addition to specialized languages for customizing the program to meet the user's needs.

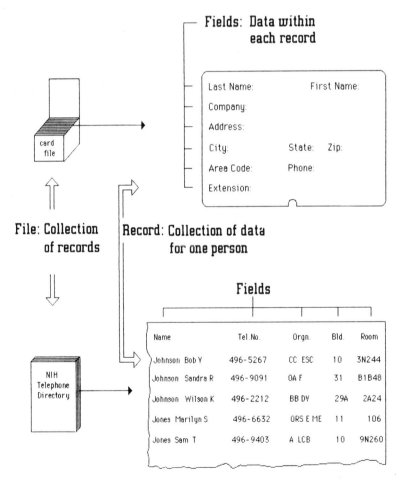

Figure 2-2

Database Capabilities

* Fast sorting of records on multiple fields.

* Fast search for specific record or records

* Can accept new data fields

* Can accept new records

* Easy report generation

Figure 2-3

Spreadsheets in the Workplace

General Ledger

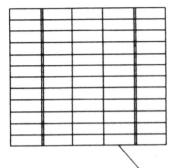

Spreadsheet Applications:

* Budget
* Procurement
* Contracts Management
* Time Management
* Project Management

Spreadsheet Capabilities:

* Automatic calculations
* Use of formulas to define relationships
* Move and copy data
* Math, financial, and statistical functions

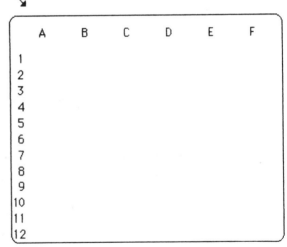

Figure 2-4

Spreadsheets

It has been said that spreadsheets were single-handedly responsible for the success of the personal computer. These claims may be exaggerated, but the impact of spreadsheet programs on business management has been nothing short of revolutionary.

As the name implies, a spreadsheet is an electronic version of a standard ledger used for decades in accounting and budgeting procedures. With this software, a "template", or form, is created, into which numbers, text, and formulas can be entered. This ability to relate values to each other and establish dependencies gives the spreadsheet its power. Changes made in one portion of the spreadsheet can be reflected throughout the sheet by using formulas to express relationships. This makes "what if" projections a simple procedure.

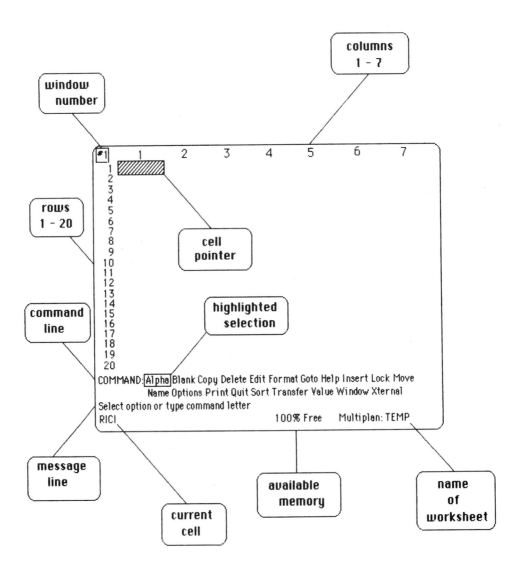

Figure 2-5

Graphics

Graphics programs have become popular recently as a result of the success of the spreadsheet. Once business executives could work with figures on an electronic spreadsheet, it was only natural to want an electronic representation in the form of a pie chart or bar graph. Graphics programs were among the first integrated programs in that they used data from another program to produce their charts and graphs. Today there are whole families of software that interchange data among their various components.

Graphics programs have also been created to allow artists and engineers to produce drawings electronically. Computer- aided design (CAD) has revolutionized the aircraft and automobile industries.

Communications

Communication programs enable microcomputers to "connect" to other microcomputers or to mainframe computers for the purposes of viewing information stored in the remote computer or transferring information to or from the remote computer. In addition to appropriate software, communication between computers requires that both the sending (transmitting) and receiving computers have a modem, a peripheral device that translates data from the transmitting computer into data that can be carried over telephone lines and translates the telephone-line data back into computer-useable data at the receiving end.

Computer communications have varied uses. Writers working at home can transmit drafts to editors, perhaps even in other cities. Through communication with bulletin board systems, users can access volumes of electronically stored information to, for example, view airline schedules, find a specialized bibliography, or "download" (receive) a new computer game.

Communications with Computers

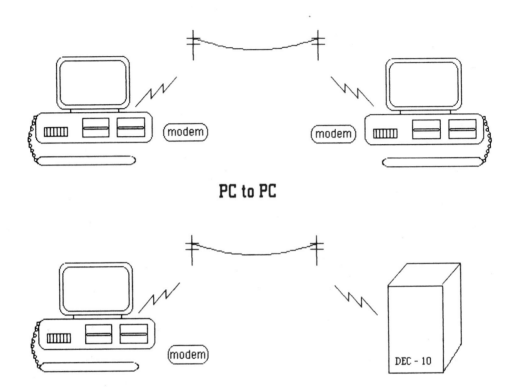

Figure 2-6

Networking

One of the newest innovations to enhance the use of computers in the workplace is the LAN—Local Area Network. Special network software and cabling can connect a number of separate computers, or workstations, to a central processing and storage device, or server. The server's large hard disk can store a single copy of each of the application programs used in the organization. Single, or multiple, printers can be connected to the server. Each workstation loads an electronic copy of a requested program from the server into its own RAM memory, rather than having a physical copy of that program on the workstation's hard disk. The workstation users can print data on the network shared printer(s), eliminating the expense of having individual printers for each computer.

In addition to sharing programs and printers, LANs allow efficient sharing of data—such as a master database for accounting purposes. Using networks with an electronic mail system enables individual workstations to send and receive memos or entire reports or spreadsheets without having to print them and without needing messenger or delivery services.

Summary—Identifying the Role of Personal Computers in the Workplace

1. Word processing—creating, editing, storing and printing text—is a major use of personal computers.

2. Desktop publishing programs allow the integration of text and graphics, as well as a wide range of formats.

3. Database management systems provide for the computerization of record-keeping functions.

4. Spreadsheet programs turn the computer into an electronic ledger, permitting the efficient manipulation of numbers.

5. Graphics packages visually represent relationships between values (graphs and chart); some of them also accommodate "freehand" drawing by the user for illustration or industrial design purposes.

6. Communication programs, in combination with modems, enable microcomputers to access data from or send data to other computers over telephone lines.

7. Networking software permits many users to share computer resources, creating more economical and efficient workplaces.

Quick Check—Identifying the Role of Personal Computers in the Workplace

Match the type of program you would use with the task you must accomplish (each type of software may apply to more than one task).

a. Word Processing

b. Desktop Publishing

c. Database Management

d. Spreadsheet

e. Graphics

f. Communications

g. Network

1. Maintaining an address list of customers

2. Sharing a laser printer among three secretaries

3. Preparing monthly budgets for several departments

4. Keeping track of subscription renewals for a magazine

5. Producing pie charts for a stockholders' report

6. Designing the entire stockholders' report

7. Drafting a memo to all department supervisors

8. Allowing the Purchasing Department and the Sales Department to update inventory records

9. Designing a company logo

10. Projecting payroll costs for several different hiring proposals

11. Sending a draft of a report across town to a reviewer for comments

UNIT·3·

Introduction to the DOS Operating System

Overview Regardless of the application for which you use your computer, you will always need DOS (or the new operating system OS/2), since your computer is powerless to perform any task without it. All applications, from word processing to database management, rely on DOS to accomplish their purpose. If you have used a computer in any capacity, you have already used DOS.

This unit presents basic operating system concepts and introduces fundamental DOS commands. You will learn how to instruct DOS to perform file, disk, and hardware operations to enable you to have greater control over your own computer environment.

Topics: Operating Systems

MS-DOS and PC-DOS

DOS Filenames

Controlling DOS

DOS Housekeeping Commands

DOS File and Disk Management Commands

Redirecting Input and Output

Pipes and Filters

Operating Systems

One part of the systems software is the "disk operating system" (referred to as DOS), which is a collection of programs that translates the user requirements into the actual equipment operations. The operating system directs all of the computer's input/output, manages the files stored on the disks and disk space allocation, and controls the allocation and interaction of all the computer's resources. The operating system is an integral part of the computer system and must be present in the computer's memory.

The operating system for a particular microcomputer is determined by the microprocessor type, since the operating system interacts directly with the microprocessor units.

When the computer is turned on, a set of instructions stored within a semiconductor, referred to as "read only memory," or ROM, is activated. It tells the computer to search for and attempt to copy the operating system from a disk into the computer's main memory. The instructions within the ROM are placed there at the time of the computer's manufacture. ROM is referred to as "read only memory" because the instructions in ROM can be read and executed only, and cannot be altered by the user. If the operating system is not present when the instructions from ROM attempt to locate it and copy it, an error message will appear on the screen requesting the user to place a disk containing the operating system in the appropriate disk drive. When ROM has copied the operating system into the computer's memory, the user can then begin to communicate with the operating system to load and execute programs or perform other tasks.

DOS and Beyond

MS-DOS was developed by the Microsoft Corporation as an operating system for computers based on the Intel 8086 and 8088 series of microprocessors. IBM calls its version of this operating system for its line of microcomputers PC-DOS.

As with any program, changes, modifications, and extensions which improve the program are made periodically. Improved versions of DOS have generally been released when new or improved hardware became available. The major changes in DOS were:

Version	Year	Major New Features
1.0	1981	original DOS
1.1	1982	double-sided disks, date, time stamping
2.0	1983	hard disk support (IBM XT) directories, filters, I/O redirection
2.1	1983	IBM PCjr support
3.0	1984	high-capacity floppy support (IBM AT)
3.1	1985	IBM PC-Net support
3.2	1986	enhanced data protection support for 3 1/2-inch disks
3.3	1987	increased serial port support; additional BACKUP, PATH and ATTRIB capabilities; better access to large-disk storage
4.0	projected	pull-down menu interface; support for extended memory; support for larger hard disks

OS/2

OS/2	1988	multitasking, enhanced memory usage

DOS Filename Rules

One of DOS's major functions is to keep track of how and where your data is stored on a disk, allowing DOS to retrieve it for you in the future. You create data—a memo, a chapter, a spreadsheet, an entire database—with an application program such as a word processor (for example, WordPerfect), an electronic spreadsheet (for example, LOTUS 1-2-3), a database management system (for example, dBASE III Plus), or a variety of other types of software. When you finish creating your data, you store it on a disk. You are asked to give your data a name under which it will be saved. DOS in effect "files" your data under that name in an appropriate place on the disk. DOS keeps a directory—a table of contents—of the names of all the files on the disk. Regardless of which application you use to create your files, DOS handles their storage and retrieval.

DOS filenames must follow these rules:

1. The filename itself may be one to eight alphanumeric characters.

2. The filename may have a three-character extension separated from the filename by a period, for a total of eleven characters.

3. Spaces and most symbols are not valid filename characters, with the exception of the underline (_) and the hyphen (-).

4. Device names used by the system—such as PRN, CON, or COM1—may not be used as a filename or extension.

5. Many software programs automatically assign extensions to their files, for example, LOTUS 1-2-3 assigns .WK1 to worksheet files, dBase III assigns .DBF to database files, and DisplayWrite4 assigns .TXT to its textfiles.

Examples:

Legal filenames	FILE	
	F2	
	MYDATA.TXT	
	PROGRAM7.PAS	
Illegal filenames	HI THERE.FIL	(space is an illegal character)
	LETTERTOJOHN	(more than eight characters)
	MYDATA.TEXT	(more than three characters in extension
	CON	(CON is a device name—refers to the console)

DOS, too, assigns special extensions to important types of files. The special DOS extensions are listed below:

Extension	Example	Meaning
.COM	COMMAND.COM BASICA.COM	command files—programs which may be called (loaded into RAM and executed) by just typing the filename without the extension
.EXE	SORT.EXE FIND.EXE	executable programs—called by just typing filename without the extension
.BAT	MENU.BAT	batch files—programs called by just typing the filename
.BAS	PROG1.BAS	BASIC program files

DOS Global Filename Characters

DOS also has two "wildcard" characters that can be inserted to represent all or part of a filename for copying, deleting, or viewing groups of files. This is very handy in backing up, and in grouping files for permanent storage.

The asterisk (*) stands for any name up to the maximum number of characters in its category.

For example, *.COM refers to all filenames, up to 8 characters, on a disk whose extension is .COM. The XT*.BAT stands for all filenames on a disk up to eight characters, that start with XT and have .BAT for an extension. The *.* stands for all filenames on a disk, up to eight characters and having any (or no) extension.

The question mark (?) stands for a single character in that exact location in the filename or extension.

For example, W???.08? stands for all files with up to four characters in a filename that starts with W and has .08 plus any character in its extension.

Examples:

MYDATA?.TXT	represents any file that has a legal character where the ? appear, for example, MYDATA3.TXT, MYDATAS.TXT.
MY*.TXT	represents any file that has a name beginning with MY and a TXT extension.
FILE.*	represents any file with FILE as a name, regardless of the extension.
*.BAS	represents any filename that has BAS as an extension.
.	represents any filename. NOTE: Be careful with this command, especially when used with ERASE.

Fundamental DOS Commands

DOS is itself a large program that has many subprograms which are called with special names. From the user's point of view, these special names are the DOS commands. When DOS is booted, most of the subprograms (commands) are loaded into random-access memory (RAM) and are available for use at any time. These commands are called <u>internal</u> commands and include those that are most commonly used, for example, DIR, CLS, ERASE.

Some DOS commands are used less often (for example, FORMAT, DISKCOPY) and are not loaded into RAM upon booting DOS, thus keeping more RAM free for user programs and data. These commands reside on disk (you will see them with .COM or .EXE extensions in a directory listing) and must be loaded from disk each time they are used (by typing their name). They are known as <u>external</u> commands.

Some fundamental DOS commands are highlighted below. Some of these commands allow variations and options.

Internal Commands

DIR	Lists the filenames, lengths, and times of last update for all files on the default disk or directory
COPY	Copies a file to another file on the same or a different disk
DATE	Prompts the user to set the current date
TIME	Prompts the user to set the time
ERASE	Erases the specified file from the disk or directory
DEL	Same as ERASE
RENAME	Renames a specified filename to another name
TYPE	Displays the contents of a specified file to the screen
CLS	Clears the screen

External Commands

    FORMAT   Prepares a blank disk for use

    DISKCOPY   Copies the contents of one disk to another

    CHKDSK   Provides information about space and files on a disk as well as available computer memory.

    PRINT   Prints a list of files (max ten) to an output device (defaults to the printer) while allowing the user to continue using the system

    LABEL   Allows user to name (label) a disk

Command Options

Many commands have one or more options, called "switches," that give them greater power and flexibility. For example, DIR displays the default directory. It can be used with several variations or switches:

1. When DIR is typed by itself, it displays the filename, file length, date of creation or last update, and time of creation or last update. The whole directory is typed in one continuous list, one line per filename.

2. DIR/P displays all the same information as above, but only one screen (page) at a time. When the screen is full, the display stops. You may display the next screenful by pressing any character.

3. DIR/W displays only the filenames contained in the directory, without the other information. It displays them in multiple columns across the width of the screen (W stands for "width" or "wide.") In this way, you can see the filenames contained in even a very long directory at a glance, all on one screen.

Controlling DOS

DOS is a command-driven system. The user types ("enters") the DOS commands via the keyboard and activates it by pressing the Return (Enter) key. DOS responds to the user's command by performing the requested action. Some commands produce "output" as the requested action—for example, DIR requests DOS to show a listing of the names of all the files in the default directory (location). Some commands do not result in visible output—for example, COPY requests DOS to duplicate a file from one disk to another. In such cases, the RESULT of the command is the copied filed; the OUTPUT of the command is the message "1 file copied."

Special keys or combinations of keys are used to control the output of DOS during DOS commands, or after they are initiated.

[Backspace]	moves cursor back a space, erasing the character
[Ctrl][Alt][Del]	reboots the system
[Ctrl][C]	breaks program or batch file
[Ctrl][S]	freezes output until a key is pressed
[Shift][PrtSc]*	dumps copy of current screen to printer
[Ctrl][PrtSc]	sends all further output to printer

---

*On keyboards that have a separate, stand-alone [PrtSc] (Print Screen) key it is not necessary to press [Shift].

"Booting Up"

"Booting" the computer means turning it on and activating ROM—Read-Only Memory. ROM has three instructions:

(1) perform a <u>POST</u>—Power On Self Test—to check and report problems with all components of the system;

(2) <u>find DOS</u>—If there is a disk in the A: drive (the left or top or only floppy disk drive), ROM assumes the DOS boot programs are on it. If DOS is not present on the disk in the A: drive (if, for example, the disk contains only user data), the boot process will halt and the message "Non-system disk in drive A: Replace and strike any key to continue" will appear. If drive A: is empty on booting, ROM will look on drive C:, the hard disk, for DOS. On a hard disk system, drive C: is where DOS is stored;

(3) <u>load DOS</u>—ROM will place an electronic copy of the DOS boot programs (COMMAND.COM, which contains instructions for implementing DOS internal commands, and the hidden programs IBMDOS.COM and IBMBIO.COM, which control system integration) into RAM. Once DOS is loaded into RAM, the user can communicate with the system. DOS will remain in RAM until the computer is turned off. The boot process is repeated each time the computer is turned on.

Unit III 37

Activity 3-1: Getting Started

(For a dual floppy system, go to APPENDIX A.)

Task	Procedure/Response
Power up (boot) the system: Wait for a POST.	Turn on the computer and monitor.
Do not place a disk in A: until the computer has booted.	
NOTE: On some computers you will see numbers incrementing at the top of your screen. This is the part of the POST called the RAM check—checking all the memory chips.	
NOTE: After the POST, DOS is automatically loaded into RAM.	
Notice the default (assumed) date. Is it correct?	_____
What is the format in which the date is displayed?	_____
Enter the date in the proper format.	mm-dd-yy[Return]
Notice the default time. Is it correct?	_____
What is the format in which the time is displayed?	_____
Enter the time in the proper format.	hh:mm[Return]
What do you see on the screen?	_____
The default drive, C, and the greater-than symbol are the default DOS prompt.	

Task

Procedure/Response

The small blinking underline is the <u>cursor</u>. It marks the position where typed characters will appear on the screen.

Place your student disk in drive A: and close the drive door.

Activity 3-2: DOS Housekeeping Commands

DOS has a number of commands that can be used to give the operator additional information and control. If you have booted your computer and bypassed the date and time, you can enter or edit them from the DOS prompt. DOS commands can be entered in upper- or lowercase letters.

Task	Procedure/Response
REMINDER: Always press [Return] when you finish typing a command. This is DOS's signal to execute the command.	
Verify the date.	DATE
Accept the new default.	[Return]
Verify the time.	TIME
Accept the new default.	[Return]
NOTE: DOS uses a 24-hour clock. If it is 1:00 pm, enter 13:00.	
Clear all this data from the screen.	CLS
Determine the version of DOS you are using.	VER
What version is it?	_____
Determine if this disk has a label.	VOL
What is the volume label?	_____
Determine if your student disk has a label.	VOL A:

Task	**Procedure/Response**

NOTE: DOS assumed you wanted the label of the disk in the default drive when you just entered VOL. You must override that assumption if you want the label of the disk in drive A:.

Name your student disk (DOS 3.0 and greater only)   LABEL A:

If you had just typed LABEL, what disk would you be naming?   _____

You may use up to eleven characters, including spaces. Upper- or lowercase is acceptable.

What volume label did you give your disk?   _____

Confirm your new volume label.   LABEL A:

What message is displayed?   _____

Respond to the message, but do not delete your label.   [Return] N

Activity 3-3: Displaying A Disk's Contents: DIR CHKDSK

The files stored on a disk are listed in the directory. The DIR command not only displays the names of the files but their size, date, and time of creation. In addition, DIR lists the amount of available space on your disk. The CHKDSK command gives information about disk space in addition to the amount of total and available memory. The initial <u>default disk drive</u> is the disk from which DOS was loaded into RAM.

You must press the [Return] or [Enter] key to activate a DOS command.

<u>Task</u>	<u>Procedure/Response</u>
Clear the screen.	CLS
Display the directory of the default disk.	DIR
You are viewing the contents of which disk?	_____
Stop/start the directory from scrolling.	DIR [Ctrl][S]
View the directory in screens.	DIR/P
Display a wide directory.	DIR/W
Look for a specific file.	DIR COMMAND.COM
Display the directory of your student disk.	DIR A:
How many files are named in this directory?	_____
What is the volume label?	_____
Look for a specific file on your student disk.	DIR A:READ.ME
If you did not include A:, on which disk would DOS look for the READ.ME file?	_____

Task	Procedure/Response
How does the directory listing separate a file name from its extension?	_____
What must you type to separate a file name from its extension?	_____
Display a group of files.	DIR A:*.COM DIR A:*.TXT
Where are these files?	_____
What is the default drive?	_____
How many .TXT files are there?	_____
Change the default to the A: drive.	A:
How has the DOS prompt changed?	_____
View the default directory.	DIR
Which disk's directory are you viewing?	_____
How would you now request a directory of drive C:?	_____
View all the .EXE files on the default drive.	DIR *.EXE
How does DOS respond if there are no files with the name you requested?	_____
Check the disk and memory status.	CHKDSK
What disk are you checking?	_____
Check the hard disk.	CHKDSK C:

On Your Own

Write the complete command you would use to accomplish the tasks. Execute the command to answer the questions.

Task	Procedure	Response
What day of the week will July 4, 1990, be?	_____	_____
Return the default date to today.	_____	
How many bytes does COMMAND.COM occupy on drive C:?	_____	_____
What time was MEMO.TXT stored on your student disk?	_____	_____
How much space is left on your student disk?	_____	_____
How many hidden files are on your student disk?	_____	_____
Delete the volume label from your student disk.	_____	
How many hidden files are there now?	_____	_____
What did the hidden file contain?		_____
Restore your volume label.	_____	

The COPY Command

The DOS COPY command is a powerful and flexible program for transferring files between disks, between system devices, and for backing up files to the same disk. It can also be used to create files and to merge several files into one. COPY does not affect the original file, but simply makes an exact copy. The COMP (Compare) command is used to verify the accuracy of the copy when very important data is being transferred. COPY does not indicate that a file of the same name exists on the target disk; therefore, it is possible to write over a file by accident.

When using COPY the following rules apply:

- The source disk is the disk you are copying FROM.

- The target disk is the disk you are copying TO.

- If no drive is specified for the source or for the target drive, COPY copies from and to the current (default) drive.

- If you are backing up a file to the same disk, you must change the name of the file or the file extension, since two files with identical names cannot exist on the same disk.

    Example: A>COPY MEMO OLDMEMO
               A>COPY MEMO MEMO.BAK

- If a file has an extension, that extension must be used in the COPY command; otherwise you will get the "File not found" error message.

- Spaces are used in COPY to separate the source file from the target file. As with all DOS commands, do not use a space between the drive designator and the file name.

    Example: A>COPY B:MEMO A:OLDMEMO

    In this example, you would not be required to include the A: designator since the default drive is A; however, using drive designators clarifies exactly what is happening in the COPY procedure.

- If you simply want to rename a file and not produce a second copy, use the RENAME command, that is, RENAME MEMO OLDMEMO. After this command, the file MEMO will no longer exist.

Activity 3-4: Copying and Verifying Files: COPY COMP

Task	Procedure/Response
Make sure drive A: is the default.	A:
View the contents of the student disk.	DIR
Copy MEMO.TXT to OLDMEMO.	COPY MEMO.TXT OLDMEMO
Does MEMO.TXT still exist?	_____
Make sure.	DIR MEMO.TXT
What message indicates a successful copy?	_____
Create a backup for NOTICE.	COPY NOTICE NOTICE.BAK
Verify your work.	DIR
To which disk were the two new files copied?	_____
How many files are now on your student disk?	_____
Copy all the files with the .TXT extension from the student disk to the hard disk.	COPY *.TXT C:
What disk is the assumed source?	_____
What response does DOS give when it copies a group of files?	_____
Check the copy with COMP.	COMP A:*.TXT C:*.TXT
What message does DOS display if files are identical?	_____
Confirm that all the .TXT files are now also on C:	DIR C:*.TXT

Task	Procedure/Response
Create backups for all the files with a .TXT extension.	COPY C:*.TXT C:*.BAK
If you did not type the second C:, where would the .BAK files be?	_____
Confirm that all the .BAK files were created.	DIR C:*.BAK
What first names do these files have?	_____
Rename OLDMEMO to NEWMEMO.	RENAME OLDMEMO NEWMEMO
What drive is assumed?	_____
Verify your work.	DIR

DISKCOPY and DISKCOMP

Two DOS external commands, DISKCOPY and DISKCOMP, allow you to copy the contents of an entire floppy disk (including directories if they have been made on the floppy) and then verify that the two disks are exactly alike. The DISKCOPY program formats the target disk as it copies files. Although this seems like a simpler procedure than COPY, it is used far less frequently for the following reasons:

- Since DISKCOPY formats the target disk, it is very easy to erase valuable files when you really want to add the files on the source disk to the target disk.

- Files cannot be copied to or from a fixed disk using DISKCOPY: an error message will result if this is attempted.

- Because the target disk is formatted, the version of DOS on the source disk will be transferred, which may not be what you desire.

- If the source disk has undergone a great deal of file creation and deletion, the diskette space will be fragmented causing delays in reading and writing on the target disk. The recommended procedure in copying these disks is to use COPY *.*, which will compress the files when they are written to the target disk.

DISKCOPY is an acceptable procedure for backing up floppy data disks for archival purposes. It is mandatory for copying directory structure; COPY *.* copies only files in the current directory. DISKCOMP is used following a DISKCOPY to verify the accuracy of the new disk.

Activity 3-5: Deleting Files: DEL ERASE

Two identical commands exist for removing files from a disk—DEL and ERASE. Both can be used to delete single files and groups of files using global and wildcard characters. Special programs like Norton Utilities can recover files that have been accidentally erased if nothing else has been written to the disk in that space. This is possible since DEL or ERASE simply deletes the file entry from the directory so that it can no longer be accessed; it does not physically erase the contents of the file from the disk. The space that the file occupied is marked as available, however; and if another file is saved over it, there is no way it can be recovered.

To erase the entire contents of a disk for reuse, use the ERASE command with global characters, ERASE *.*. You will be prompted with the following message: "Are you sure (Y/N)?" to which you must respond. This is a failsafe device, since this command will wipe out your entire disk. USE IT CAREFULLY.

Task	Procedure/Response
Erase the file NEWMEMO.	ERASE NEWMEMO
From what disk was this file erased?	_____
Delete the .TXT files copied in the previous activity.	DEL C:*.TXT
What message indicates a group of files has been deleted?	_____
Delete the .BAK files from the hard disk.	DEL C:*.BAK
Check the directory to verify the results.	DIR C:

Activity 3-6: Viewing the Contents of a File: TYPE

Text files created under DOS can be viewed on the screen or sent to the printer using the TYPE command. Files created in most word-processing programs can also be viewed using TYPE but will be difficult to read, since all formatting is lost and format characters display as extraneous symbols. The .COM and .EXE files cannot be viewed in this manner as they are not stored in "human-readable" form.

An important application of TYPE is in viewing the contents of a READ.ME file. These files are often put on purchased software to indicate updates and changes in the program that have not been included in the documentation. Always check a new program for a READ.ME file, since they generally contain valuable information.

Task	Procedure/Response
View the contents of your disk's MEMO.TXT file.	TYPE MEMO.TXT
Can you clearly read all the words?	_____
View the contents of the file named NOTICE.	TYPE NOTICE
Was NOTICE stored in a DOS-readable format?	_____
Try to view the contents of COMMAND.COM.	TYPE C:COMMAND.COM
Why can't you understand the contents?	_____
View the contents of SDIR.DOC.	TYPE SDIR.DOC
Control the scrolling.	[Ctrl][S]
Read the READ.ME file. Cancel the scrolling.	TYPE READ.ME [Ctrl][C]
Are SDIR.DOC and READ.ME DOS-readable files?	_____

Redirecting Input and Output

The standard output device is the screen or monitor. That is, the output of all commands are generally sent to the screen for viewing. The standard input device is the keyboard. DOS allows both input and output to be redirected to other than the standard devices. A file can receive the results of a command. This file could then be used with a word-processing application, for example, to become part of a larger manuscript. The printer can also be an output device, with results of commands redirected to it to allow for hardcopy output.

The following symbols redirect input/output:

>PRN   causes output of command to be directed to the printer (PRN) rather than to the monitor

>[filename]   causes file to be created and output to be directed to this file

>>[filename] causes file to be opened and output directed to end of file

<[filename]   causes input to come from file as opposed to keyboard

Activity 3-7: Redirecting Output

Task	Procedure/Response
	*** Turn on your printer before continuing ***
Send a copy of the directory of your student disk to the printer.	DIR>PRN
Store a copy of the directory in a file.	DIR>DIR.FIL
On what disk has this file been created?	_____

NOTE: This file could be read by any word-processing program; it could be edited to provide an annotated directory list.

Task	Procedure/Response
How could you view the contents of this new file?	_____
Get hard copy (printed copy) of the results of the CHKDSK command.	CHKDSK>PRN
Print a copy of the file SDIR.DOC.	TYPE SDIR.DOC>PRN

Using Pipes and Filters

Piping allows the standard output of one program to be used as the standard input to another program. Temporary files are created in the root directory to hold the data being piped. The pipe symbol is the broken vertical line above the backslash on the lower-left side of the keyboard. In this manual it will appear as a solid line (|).

A filter is a program or command that reads data from a standard input device, modifies the data, then writes the result to a standard output device. The three standard DOS filters are:

MORE — breaks output (typically from the TYPE command) into screen-sized units for display

SORT — sorts data alphabetically

FIND — searches output for a specific string of characters and displays only those lines which contain that string

By combining redirection, pipes, and filters, the output of one program, for example, TYPE, is piped (|) to the filter program which performs an action on it and delivers the result to the screen, printer, or another file as directed. These filters can also be used as stand-alone commands.

Activity 3-8: Variations on TYPE: Pipes and Filters

Task	Procedure/Response
View the contents of the READ.ME file.	TYPE READ.ME
View the contents of this file one screen at a time.	TYPE READ.ME|MORE
What message indicates that you should continue?	_____
How can you continue?	_____
Find a specific character string in the SDIR.DOC file.	TYPE SDIR.DOC|FIND "sort"
Are only lines containing the distinct word "sort" found?	_____
How many lines in SDIR.DOC contain the characters "sort"?	_____
Find a specific character string in the MEMO.TXT file.	TYPE MEMO.TXT|FIND "EDLIN"
Try to find lines of output that contain the characters "Edlin".	TYPE MEMO.TXT|FIND "Edlin"
Is case significant to the FIND filter?	_____
Print the lines that contain "EDLIN".	TYPE MEMO.TXT|FIND "EDLIN">PRN
Display the contents of WORDS.TXT.	TYPE WORDS.TXT
Sort the file alphabetically by first character of each line.	TYPE WORDS.TXT|SORT
Redirect the output of the above command to a file.	TYPE WORDS.TXT|SORT>WORDSORT.TXT

| **Task** | **Procedure/Response** |

View the contents of the new file.   TYPE WORDSORT.TXT

How could you print the contents?   _____

Has WORDS.TXT been changed?   _____

Verify your answer.   TYPE WORDS.TXT

See the directory entry for the new file.   DIR *.TXT

When was it created?   _____

Send an alphabetically sorted directory to the printer.   DIR|SORT>PRN

NOTE: The first two numbered files are temporary files created by the SORT filter.

Send a directory sorted in descending order (reverse).   DIR|SORT/R>PRN

Sort the directory by file size.   DIR|SORT/+16

NOTE: This version of SORT rearranges each line of output according to the 16th character on each line. In some lines, the 16th character is blank or a character other than a number.

On Your Own—DOS Basics

Task	Procedure	Response
Turn off the computer if it is on.		
Boot up.	_____	
Respond to DATE and TIME prompts.	_____	
Print a directory of the default drive.	_____	
Change the default drive to the one containing your student disk.	_____	
Print out the text of WORDSORT.TXT.	_____	
Change the name of WORDSORT.TXT to SORTLIST.	_____	
Must all DOS-readable files have a .TXT extension?		_____
Does renaming a file change its date?	_____	_____
Copy COMMAND.COM from the hard disk to your student disk.	_____	
Does copying a file change its date?	_____	_____
Make the boot disk the default.	_____	
View an alphabetical listing of the default directory.	_____	
If two files have the same first name, which one does SORT alphabetize first?		_____
What comes first in SORTed order, numbers or letters?		_____
Are spaces alphabetized before or after numbers?		_____

Task	Procedure	Response
Choose a file on your student disk and make a backup copy of it on the same disk.	_____	

Summary—DOS Basics

1. DOS commands are actually subprograms within the larger program of DOS itself.

2. A legal DOS filename:

    - can have no more than eight characters, plus an optional three--character extension.

    - can contain only alphanumeric characters—no spaces and only the hyphen or underline symbol.

    - cannot use extensions reserved for system or program files (.COM, .EXE, and so on).

3. DOS contains two global filename characters:

    * stands for one or more characters at the position indicated in a filename.

    ? stands for exactly one character, for each ? typed, at the position indicated in a filename.

4. DOS actions can be controlled with various keystrokes and combinations of keystrokes.

5. The DIR command can be modified with the switches /P and /W to change how the directory is viewed.

6. Both DIR and CHKDSK give you information about storage on your disk; only CHKDSK gives information about memory use.

7. DOS output can be redirected to a file or to the printer instead of the standard output device, the monitor.

8. Both DEL and ERASE can be used to remove files from a disk.

9. The TYPE command is used to view the contents of a DOS-readable text file. It is not possible to read a .COM or an .EXE file.

10. The COPY command creates a duplicate of the source file on the target location.

11. RENAME changes one file name to another. It does not affect the content, size, or date of the file.

12. DOS FILTERS receive output from a command, manipulate that output, and display the results.

13. The MORE filter displays output from the TYPE command one screen at a time.

14. The FIND filter displays only those lines of output from the TYPE command that contain the specified characters.

15. The SORT filter rearranges lines of output from the TYPE command into the specified order. The default order is alphabetically by first character of each line.

16. The term "default" represents an assumed condition—what the computer assumes to be true unless you tell it something else. The default drive is the current drive, represented by the DOS prompt.

Quick Check—DOS Basics

1. How can a disk's directory be sent to the printer?

2. When would you use global filename characters?

3. What are two versions of a command that allow you to view a directory listing?

4. What is the difference between internal and external commands?

5. What is the result of ERASE *.*?

6. How do you know which is the current or default drive?

UNIT·4·

Additional External Commands

Overview: DOS includes a number of separate utility programs (with .COM extensions) that enhance the user's control over hardware and files. These programs are stored on disk and are loaded into RAM when the user requests them by typing their name. The program executes and then is automatically removed from RAM. These separate DOS programs are also called DOS external commands.

Topics:
PRINT

RECOVER

ATTRIB

CHKDSK/V and CHKDSK/F

ASSIGN

MODE

The PRINT Command

The DOS PRINT command sends the contents of from one to ten files to the printer. The difference between using PRINT and using TYPE is that PRINT operates in the background, which means you can use your computer for other tasks while the named files are printing.

The first time during each work session that you PRINT a file, the resident portion of the program will be loaded, thus increasing the memory required by DOS. You will also be given a chance to designate the printer port to which you want the output sent. Pressing [Return] accepts the parallel port.

Example: A>PRINT FILE1 FILE2 FILE3 FILE4

will send the four named files to the printer.

The global filename characters * and ? are allowed, thus enabling the printing of groups of files at one time.

Options available with PRINT include the following:

- PRINT/T   cancels printing of all files in queue.

- PRINT filename/C   cancels named file.

- PRINT   lists name of files, if any, in the print queue.

Activity 4-1: PRINT

Task	Procedure
	*** Turn on the printer ***
Be sure your student disk is the default.	
Send the contents of your .DOC files to the printer.	PRINT *.DOC
Continue using DOS while printing.	[Return]
List the names of the files in the print queue.	PRINT
Remove SDIR.DOC from the queue.	PRINT SDIR.DOC/C
Confirm that it has been removed.	PRINT

The RECOVER Command

The RECOVER command allows the user to partially or completely recover a file that may have been accidentally left "open" at a sudden power loss, if the application software being used at the time does not have the ability to handle such a problem.

The command also allows you to recover files from a disk that has a bad sector. Although you can recover the file, the data in the bad sector cannot be recovered. If the disk directory has been damaged, use RECOVER to recover the entire disk of files.

<u>Example</u>: A>RECOVER B:MEMO.TXT

        A>RECOVER A:

The recovered text file may need to be edited to remove unwanted data added during the recovery process. When all the files on a disk are recovered, each file will be listed in the directory as follows:

    FILE####.REC where #### is a sequential number
                     beginning with 0001.

If only one file was recovered, it can be edited from within the application which created it. If the entire disk was recovered because of damage to the directory, each .REC file should be viewed to try to determine its contents and therefore its old name. This can be a tedious process, but well worth it if most, if not all, of the files can be made useable again.

The ATTRIB Command

The ATTRIB command allows you to set or reset the READ-ONLY file attribute or to view the current attribute setting, thus protecting vital files. It is very easy to protect your valuable files—such as AUTOEXEC.BAT, CONFIG.SYS, or batch files—from accidental or unauthorized editing or erasing by employing this command.

The syntax of this command is: ATTRIB +R <filename>

Groups of files can be protected with: ATTRIB +R *.TXT
                                            ATTRIB +R *.*

To display the current attribute
setting: ATTRIB <filename>

Activity 4-2: ATTRIB

Task	Procedure
Make the file MEMO.TXT read-only.	ATTRIB +R MEMO.TXT
Display the read-only attribute of all the .TXT files.	ATTRIB *.TXT
How does DOS identify read-only files?	_____
Display the contents of MEMO.TXT.	TYPE MEMO.TXT
Can you see its contents?	_____
Attempt to copy another file to a file called MEMO.TXT.	COPY NOTICE MEMO.TXT
What would happen to the original MEMO.TXT if the copy had been successful?	_____
Try to erase MEMO.TXT.	ERASE MEMO.TXT
What message indicates the file cannot be deleted?	_____
Copy MEMO.TXT to a new file.	COPY MEMO.TXT MEMO2.TXT
Try to erase MEMO2.TXT	ERASE MEMO2.TXT
Are attributes copied with files?	_____
Remove the read-only attribute.	ATTRIB -R MEMO.TXT

The CHKDSK Command

You have already used CHKDSK to find out how much disk space is available. In this way, you can avoid losing data by being sure you have enough space for the data you want to enter onto disk.

The CHKDSK command can also be used to ensure the integrity of file structures by analyzing directories, files, and the File Allocation Table, report hidden files, and produce a memory status report.

```
A>CHKDSK                            A>CHKDSK B:

  362496 bytes total disk space       362496 bytes total disk space
   22528 bytes in 3 hidden files           0 bytes in 1 hidden files
    3072 bytes in 3 directories      274432 bytes in 15 user files
  139264 bytes in 26 user files       32768 bytes in bad sectors
  197632 bytes available on disk      55296 bytes available on disk

  524288 bytes total memory          524288 bytes total memory
  215952 bytes free                  215952 bytes free
```

Several parameters give additional power and capabilities to the CHKDSK command:

/V   displays all files and their paths on the default or specified drive.

/F   fixes errors in the directory or file allocation table and writes the corrections to disk.

filename   reports number of non-contiguous blocks in specified file.

.   reports number of noncontiguous blocks for all files in the current directory.

Files with many noncontiguous blocks take longer to load because they are spread out over the disk. If CHKDSK *.* reports a file is not contiguous, copy it to another position on disk by copying it under a different name. See if that file is contiguous with CHKDSK <new filename>. If this new file is contiguous, delete the old file and rename the new one to the original name.

If CHKDSK encounters lost clusters, the system will ask if the lost data or clusters should be converted into files. When the user answers "Y" the system will place the recovered data into a file. The user can find out the name the system has given to the file by looking in the directory. System-recovered files are usually named like this:

FILE0001.CHK

Activity 4-3: Checking Disk Validity

Task	Procedure
For a dual floppy system, go to Appendix B).	
Be sure the default drive contains your student disk.	A:
At the prompt, tell the computer to check the disk.	CHKDSK
The program may tell you it has found lost clusters. If so, it will ask: CONVERT LOST CHAINS TO FILES (Y/N)?	Y
If there were lost clusters, take a look at them:	DIR *.CHK
Display a listing of all the file names.	CHKDSK/V
Which is the hidden file?	_____
What do you think it contains?	_____
Check the integrity of all the files in the directory.	CHKDSK *.*
If a file is reported noncontiguous, copy it to a file with a different name. CHKDSK that file. It should now be contiguous. Delete the original file and rename the new file with the original name.	
Check the hard disk.	CHKDSK C:
Display a listing of all the files on the hard disk.	CHKDSK C:/V
Be prepared to suspend the scrolling.	[Ctrl][S]

Task   **Procedure**

What are the names of the two hidden
boot files near the beginning of the
list?   _____

Notice the large number of file names you did not see with the DIR command. These files are in different groupings (called subdirectories) on the hard disk. We will explore these later.

The ASSIGN Command

The ASSIGN command allows you to reroute a request for a read or write from one disk drive to another.

One of the major uses of ASSIGN is to redirect reads and writes from the default specified in purchased software. Al-though many programs have installation procedures that allow you to assign the drive where your data or program disk can be found, others do not. If a program lacks this capability, you can route the request to your preferred drive with the ASSIGN command.

ASSIGN A=C   sends all program request for the A drive to the C drive.

ASSIGN   resets drive assignments to original defaults.

If you have set up a temporary disk in RAM, you might use the ASSIGN command to route requests to it instead of reinstalling your program.

The MODE Command

MODE is an external DOS command that sets a method of operation for printers, monitors, and asynchronous communications devices (for example, modems, serial printers). This command actually sets defaults in the interface boards for the various devices.

Printers

For parallel printers, you can select one of three printer ports, and, if you have an IBM dot-matrix graphics (or compatible) printer, the number of characters per line (80 or 132), and the number of lines per inch of vertical spacing (6 or 8).

The default set upon booting is printer 1, 80 characters per line, and 6 lines per inch, that is, MODE LPT1:80,6

Example: To change the printer mode to 132 characters per line (compressed output) use this command:

> MODE LPT1:132,6

For serial printers (for example, some letter-quality printers and a few dot-matrix printers) the mode must be used to specify which communications port is used.

Example: To set defaults for a serial printer that must be attached through the serial port #1 of the asynchronous communications adapter (the color/printer adapter communicates in parallel), use this command:

> MODE LPT1:=COM1
> MODE COM1:12,N,7,1,P

Asynchronous Communications Adapter

The asynchronous communications adapter options set includes: communication port (1 or 2), baud rate, parity, databits, and stopbits.

For using an information utility like the SOURCE or CompuServe with a 1200 BAUD modem, the following would be given:

MODE COM1:12,N,8,1

This sets the defaults to port 1, 1200 BAUD, no parity, 8 databits, and 1 stopbit.

ACTIVITY 4-4: MODE

The MODE command can also be used to change the default appearance of the monitor.

The display unit can be set for number of characters per line (40 or 80), color or monochrome, and adjusted right or left.

Task	Procedure
Change the monitor to display 40 characters per line.	MODE 40
What difference do you notice?	_____
Return to 80 characters per line.	MODE 80
Shift the display one character to the right.	MODE 80,R
Shift to the right a few (at least six) more times.	MODE ,R or MODE 80,R MODE ,R MODE ,R
Check the alignment of your display.	MODE ,L,T or MODE 80,L,T and MODE ,R,T

[Note: The 80 in the above commands is optional; however, the comma which would come after the 80 must be typed.]

Try the following, if you have an IBM or IBM-compatible dot-matrix printer:

Task	Procedure
Set the printer to print in compressed mode.	MODE LPT1:132
Print a copy of SORTLIST	TYPE SORTLIST >PRN
Set the printer's vertical spacing to eight lines per inch.	MODE LPT1:,8
Again print WORDSORT.TXT	TYPE WORDSORT.TXT >PRN

On Your Own — Additional External Commands

Task	Procedure	Response
Be sure the student disk is the default.		
Display the directory of your student disk on a 40-character screen.	_____	
Change the MODE back to 80 if you prefer, or leave it at 40.		
Determine the total amount of RAM your computer has.	_____	_____
How much is used by the operating system?	_____	_____
Using two different commands, determine the amount of space remaining on your student disk.	_____	_____
	_____	_____
Do the two numbers agree?		_____
Protect all the .DOC files on your student disk from accidental erasure.	_____	
View the attributes of all the files on your student disk.	_____	
How many files are Read-only?		_____
Suppose you had tried to TYPE the READ.ME file and had seen a lot of extraneous "garbage" characters on the screen. The file seemed to be shorter than it should be. How would you try to fix it?	_____	
How many bytes recover successfully?		_____

Challenge:

Print the names of all the .COM files
on your boot disk, including the
hidden files.   _____

The three .COM files on your student disk are utility programs which are not part of DOS but which use and expand upon DOS commands. Read the documentation that comes with two of them. They are loaded just like DOS external commands (by typing their name). Experiment with all three. Which DOS command does each enhance? Read the screen for additional information while these programs are executing.

Summary—Additional External Commands

1. The PRINT external command allows the contents of up to ten files to be printed while freeing the computer for other uses.

2. CHKDSK checks a hard disk or floppy disk for data errors. It also displays how much space is in use both in RAM and on the disk, what kinds of files are on the disk, and how much space remains. With the /V switch, it lists all the files, including hidden files, in all subdirectories. With the /F option, it can recover lost data or clusters into a file. The commands CHKDSK *.* or CHKDSK <filename> display the number of noncontiguous blocks in all or the specified file. Files with many noncontiguous blocks can often be recombined by copying them to another location on the disk.

3. RECOVER closes files left open when power to the computer was lost. It will also recover one or more files from a disk that has bad sectors. It cannot recover data that was stored in bad sectors, nor can it retrieve data that was in RAM but had not been saved when the power went off. Check the contents of a recovered file for missing data.

4. The ATTRIB command enables the user to mark a file or group of files as Read-only. Read-only files can be viewed with the TYPE command, or they can be retrieved to be read in a word processing program; but they cannot be changed or deleted.

5. ASSIGN reroutes requests from one drive to another.

6. The MODE command allows you to set the default for monitors, communications devices, and selected printers.

Quick Check—Additional External Commands

1. When and how are external commands loaded into RAM?

2. What is the major advantage of the PRINT command? Can you use it to print all the files created by any word processor?

3. Does the ATTRIB +R command prevent a file from being copied?

4. How could you print a complete directory containing 80 files on a single piece of paper (that can accommodate 66 standard lines of text) if you had an IBM graphics-compatible printer?

UNIT·5·

Disk Organization

Overview: Most computers used today have a hard disk for file storage. Many of today's powerful and sophisticated application programs are too large to fit on a single 360 Kb floppy. They are written on multiple floppies. It is inconvenient and time consuming to run these programs from floppies. They can be copied to hard disks, which have much greater capacity, and executed much more efficiently.

Hard disks are used not only for storing programs but also as a convenient "file cabinet" for the files created by those programs. But with convenience can also come disorganization. The large capacity of hard disks—20, 30, 40 or more million bytes—necessitates a system for organizing the storage of files. Just as you wouldn't "file" paper documents wherever they happened to land in a file cabinet, neither is it good practice to store electronic files haphazardly on a large disk. Lack of organization results in lost time and, often, lost files.

This unit explores DOS commands that allow the user to arrange and maintain a hard disk like a well-organized file cabinet, grouping files together in a logical way so that they can easily be retrieved.

Topics: Formatting Disks

Physical Organization

Logical Organization

Creating Subdirectories

Managing Subdirectories

PROMPT

PATH

SUBST

The FORMAT Command

Disks—floppy or hard—must be formatted before they can be used. The FORMAT command organizes the disk for reading and writing under DOS. It reserves special places on the disk to hold the directory and the File Allocation Table that holds information about the actual location of files on the disk.

A disk formatted under one operating system cannot be read from or written to under another operating system; thus the impossibility of transporting disks between computers with different operating systems.

Formatting permanently removes any data stored on the disk. Usually only brand-new disks are formatted, so the erasure of data is irrelevant. However, occasionally it is necessary to reformat a floppy or even a hard disk because the disk has been damaged or the directory has been corrupted. In such cases all files should be copied to another disk, if possible, before reformatting. Remember, EVERYTHING ON THE DISK WILL BE LOST.

FORMAT allows two basic options, or switches, /S and /V.

The /S switch transfers the DOS system to the disk, thus making it a "bootable" disk. The system files are COMMAND.COM, IBMDOS.COM, and IBMBIO.COM. They take up from 40 to 60 K on the disk, depending on the version of DOS. The first two are "hidden files" and do not appear in a directory listing. Unless you need a bootable disk, adding the system is not recommended, as it substantially decreases the amount of storage available for your files.

The /V switch allows a volume name to be entered for the disk. This would provide identification if a label were lost or removed from a disk. This name is kept in a hidden file, which also takes up space. In earlier versions of DOS this name could only be given when a disk was formatted; subsequent versions (3.0 and later) have a LABEL command to add or alter a volume name at any time.

High-density floppy disks can be formatted with an additional switch, /4, that formats them as if they were standard 360 Kb double-density disks, allowing them to be read and written to in a double-density drive.

Physical Organization

Physical organization is how the computer views the disk. Floppy disks formatted for DOS use a scheme illustrated below.

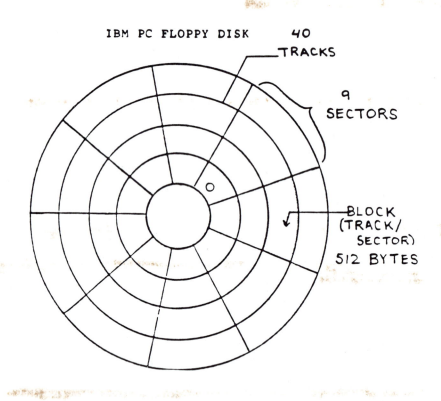

Figure 5-1

DOS uses both sides of the disk. For each disk:

2 sides X 40 tracks X 9 sectors X 512 bytes/block = 368,640 bytes or 360K. The IBM AT can accept disks formatted for 1200K or 1.2 megabytes.

Hard Disk Organization

The IBM XT and compatible computers have a built in 20 megabyte or larger hard disk. A megabyte (M) is 2^{20} bytes. Just as 2^{10} bytes is rounded off and called a kilobyte, 2^{20} bytes is called a megabyte. A 20M hard disk can store about 20 million bytes (characters). The hard disk in the PC is actually composed of two metallic 5 1/4-inch disks used on both sides for a total of four surfaces. This requires four heads to read and write data, but since the disk is sealed, and rigid, tolerances can be much closer for operation. Thus, more tracks (called cylinders) and sectors can be used on the same surface area.

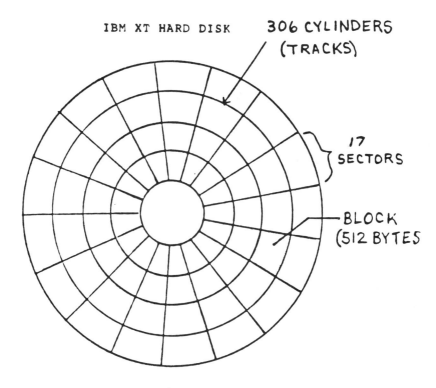

Figure 5-2

For 10 Megabyte IBM XT hard disks:

4 sides X 306 cylinders X 17 sectors X 512 bytes/block = 10,653,696 bytes of storage.

Formatting and Maintaining a Hard Disk

DO NOT Format the hard disk (if available) during this course!

There are two steps in preparing a new hard disk for use: Partitioning the disk, and formatting it. A disk may be partitioned if you will be using different operating systems with the same disk, for example, DOS and UCSD Pascal. The external command FDISK is used to partition a hard disk. After a disk has been partitioned (you must partition it even if you are using only one operating system), the FORMAT command is used to format the DOS partition. Be extremely careful using FORMAT with DOS 2.1 or earlier versions, since no confirmation is required and formatting wipes out all previous data! We will discuss a way to avoid this unpleasant experience later.

Most users include the DOS system files when preparing the hard disk (use /S after the FORMAT command), so they can boot from the hard disk which is called the C: drive. By leaving the drive A: door open, the system will look in the C: drive for DOS, and boot from it. This allows you to avoid booting from the DOS disk each time.

Logical Organization: Tree-Structured Directory

Logical organization is how the user views the disk. For floppy disks a simple directory which lists all files sequentially is usually sufficient. For high-density floppy disks and hard disks, so many files can be stored that an alternative structure for organizing filenames is needed. PC-DOS uses an inverted tree structure to group collections of files into subdirectories. The top of the tree is called the root. A disk without any subdirectories simply keeps all files in the root. The root is the default directory when DOS is booted and is indicated by the backslash (\).

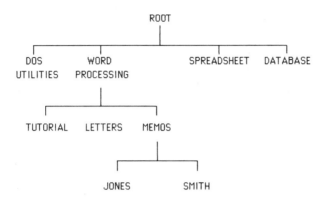

Figure 5-3

Guidelines for Creating Subdirectories

As with all computer operations, developing a plan before you begin work on the computer is invaluable. Some guidelines for creating subdirectories follow:

- Keep the structure to the most simple one that will meet your needs; do not create more levels than necessary.

- Create a subdirectory for each application just below the root. You might have any or all of the following first-level subdirectories:

  Word Processing
  Database Program
  Spreadsheet Program
  DOS files
  Batch files
  Utilities
  Communications

- Create a second level for the data files under each applications directory. For example, under Word Processing, you may want these subdirectories:

  Proposals
  Contracts
  Correspondence
  Reports
  Memos

- If your machine has multiple users, each person might have his/her own subdirectory for data used by applications.

DOS Subdirectory Commands

Internal

DIR	Lists files on default directory or directory specified in path.
MKDIR (MD)	Make Directory: Creates a new subdirectory.
CHDIR (CD)	Change Directory: Changes the default directory.
RMDIR (RD)	Remove Directory: deletes a directory. The directory must be empty before it can be deleted.
PATH	Sets a path of directories for DOS to automatically search for commands or batch files.

External

CHKDSK/V	Analyzes directories and files and reports status.
TREE	Produces an outline listing of all directories.
TREE/F	Produces an outline listing of all subdirectories and their files.
BACKUP	Copies specified hard-disk files, subdirectories, or the entire disk to floppy disks.
RESTORE	Restores files from floppy-disk backups to the hard disk.

Moving Between Directories

When you display the structure using the TREE command, each directory is shown with the following:

PATH: \<directory name>

This indicates that to get to each of these directories, you must go through the root directory (\). The \DOS can be thought of as the "address" of the DOS directory. From any place in the tree, you can get to this directory by entering its address, \DOS.

If you were in the root directory, you would type:

CD DOS

to change to the DOS directory. However, if you were in the DOS directory and wanted to go to the WORD directory, then you would type:

CD \WORD

which means go to the root directory and then to the subdirectory WORD. You cannot go directly to a subdirectory on the same level without going through the root.

There are several options to help you determine where you are in your tree-structured directory.

- Type: CD

    to display the current directory.

- Use the DOS PROMPT command to reconfigure the prompt.

    A>PROMPT PG

    will change the prompt to display the current directory ($P) along with the usual greater-than (>) symbol ($G).

    <u>Example:</u>   A:\DOS>

Activity 5-1: Navigating a Tree-Structured Directory

Moving between directories allows the user to view files stored at each location.

Task	Procedure
Make the hard disk the default.	C:
Print a list of all directories.	DIR *. >PRN

NOTE: This listing will include all files that have no extension. Directories have names, but no extensions.

Task	Procedure
Into how many directories has your hard disk been organized?	_____
Produce an outline listing of all directories.	TREE>PRN

Refer to your printed directory listing and tree outline to change into various directories.

NOTE: Directory names used here are those in general use; your names may be different.

Task	Procedure
	CD DOS
View the files in this directory.	DIR

Continue in like manner through several other directories.

REMINDER: To change into a lower-level directory, no \ is necessary. The \ means "Start back at the root." It _is_ necessary when changing to a higher-level directory or to another directory on the same level.

Task	Procedure
Verify the current directory.	CD
Return to the root directory.	CD \

Activity 5-2: Simulating A Hard Disk

In this activity you will begin setting up the floppy disk in your A: drive as if it were your new hard disk. The remainder of the activities in this course will simulate hard disk set-up and maintenance. For purposes of these exercises, "pretend" the floppy disk is your C: (hard) drive. In like manner, "pretend" the DOS programs on your current hard disk are really on a floppy disk in drive A:—as they would be on your original DOS floppy, if you were setting up a new hard disk for your computer.

Task	Procedure/Response
Copy all the files from your student disk into the root directory of C:	COPY A:*.* C:\
Create a bootable floppy disk. **REMINDER:** The A: disk is simulating your new hard disk, which would be C:.	FORMAT A:/S
Do not format any other disks.	N
How much disk space does the system require?	_____
See that COMMAND.COM has been copied as part of the /S formatting procedure.	DIR A:
How much space does COMMAND.COM require?	_____
What files are using the rest of the "system" space?	_____
View the hidden boot files on your newly formatted disk.	CHKDSK A:/V
Restart (reboot) the computer from the files on your A: disk.	[Ctrl][Alt][Del]

Task	Procedure/Response
Notice the DOS prompt; which drive is the default?	_____
Enter the date and time.	mm-dd-yy[Return] hh:mm[Return]
Execute other internal DOS commands.	VER CLS
Try to run CHKDSK	CHKDSK
What message appears?	_____

Before we rebooted with the disk in drive A: CHKDSK worked even with drive A: as the default. When we booted from drive C: a special file (one that is not yet present on your new boot disk) was executed that contained a PATH command. This command enabled DOS to find CHKDSK even if CHKDSK were not on the default disk. We will store a PATH command in a file on the A: disk later.

Without the PATH command, DOS must have explicit directions to find external commands.

Try to run the CHKDSK program again, this time including the location (path) of the program.	C:\DOS\CHKDSK

NOTE: Use the name of the directory of your C: drive in which the DOS external programs are stored.

What disk are you checking?   _____

Activity 5-3: Creating A Tree-Structured Directory

To gain experience with subdirectory commands, you will create the directory shown below.

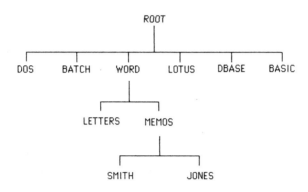

Figure 5-4

Task	Procedure/Response
Create your first subdirectory.	MD DOS
Change into the DOS subdirectory and view the contents.	CD DOS DIR
What two files are there?	_____
NOTE: "Dot" and "double dot" are DOS housekeeping files containing directory location information.	
Return to the root directory.	CD \

94   The DOS Book

Task	**Procedure/Response**
Following the tree-structured directory below, create the remaining first level directories.	

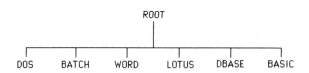

Figure 5-5

Task	Procedure/Response
Return to the root.	CD \
View your progress with the DIR command.	DIR
How are directories identified in this listing?	_____
How many directories have you made?	_____
View your directories with the TREE command.	C:\DOS\TREE
REMINDER: TREE.COM is an external command; DOS must be told where to find it.	
Change between the various directories.	CD DOS CD\WORD CD\BASIC
Why is the \ necessary to move between DOS and WORD, or between WORD and BASIC?	_____

Task	Procedure/Response
Why was the slash not necessary to move from the root to DOS?	_____
Identify the current directory.	CD
What is the default directory?	_____

The PROMPT Command

The default DOS prompt—the symbol indicating that DOS is ready to receive a command—is the current disk-drive designation followed by a "greater-than" sign: A> or C>. The PROMPT command allows the user to change that prompt to better suit his or her needs. Text can be a part of your customized prompt. Other special symbols can be incorporated into a prompt by typing a $, followed by the character which stands for a particular symbol.

Some of the options that can be included in the PROMPT command are:

    $t   time
    $d   date
    $p   current directory
    $v   version number
    $n   default drive letter
    $g   > symbol
    $_   carriage return (for a two-line prompt)
    $e   escape

Activity 5-4: Creating Customized Prompts

Task	Procedure/Response
Change your prompt to "Hello".	PROMPT Hello
What does your prompt look like?	_____
Where is the cursor?	_____
Where would you begin typing a DOS command?	_____
Add the "greater-than" symbol to separate the prompt from following commands.	PROMPT Hello$g
Change the prompt to include the current date.	PROMPT Today is dg
Construct a two-line prompt.	PROMPT Hello$_Today is dg
NOTE: The $_ inserts a carriage return and line feed into the prompt, placing all following characters on the next line.	
See the effect of using such a prompt.	DIR
Return the prompt to the default.	PROMPT
Construct a prompt to reflect the current directory.	PROMPT PG
Move between directories with the new prompt.	CD\WORD, etc.

Activity 5-5: Completing the Tree-Structured Directory

You have two choices when creating directories at a second or greater level:

- Change to the directory in which the new subdirectories are to reside and execute the make directory (MD) command.

- Write the address of the subdirectory as you create it from the root, for example, to create MEMOS in WORD, enter the following:

    MD \WORD\MEMOS

Task	Procedure/Response
Change to WORD.	CD \WORD
Create MEMOS.	MD MEMOS
Why should you <u>not</u> type MD \MEMOS?	_____
What level directory would be created with MD \MEMOS?	_____
Return to the root.	CD \
Create LETTERS from the root.	MD \ WORD\LETTERS
Check your work.	C:\DOS\TREE
Which disk's TREE are you seeing?	_____

Task	Procedure/Response

Complete the structure shown below.

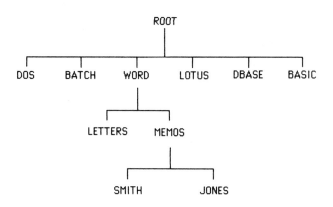

Figure 5-6

File Specification

Files are located in directories. On your original student disk, all the files were located in the root directory. There were no subdirectories. When C: was the default, we needed only to tell DOS the disk designation, if we wanted to work with a file.

As directories are created and files copied into them, we need to give DOS more information about the location of a file, if that file is not in the default directory.

File specification, or path address, tells DOS the complete and specific location of a file.

The parts of a full file specification are:

Drive Designator

Directory Name(s)

File Name

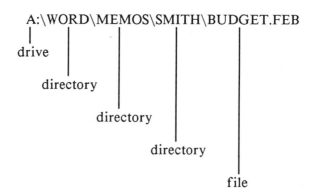

Figure 5-7

There are no spaces within the specification.

Parts of the specification are separated by backslashes. The first backslash indicates the root directory; other backslashes are simply separators. DOS assumes each part of the specification is a directory unless it can find no directory with that name, in which case it assumes it is a filename.

Activity 5-6: Copying Files Into A Subdirectory

Once you have established your subdirectories, you can use the COPY command to transfer files into each directory and between directories. Because of the copy protection found on most purchased programs, you will not copy an application like Lotus 1-2-3 in this course. Be sure to follow the procedures in the documentation for installing these program in their proper directory at your own site.

In the same way that you created subdirectories, you can copy files by changing to the destination directory or by giving the path to that directory.

Task	Procedure/Response
Copy some of the DOS files from C: into your DOS subdirectory.	CD \DOS COPY C:\DOS*.COM COPY C:\DOS*.EXE
In the above COPY commands what does the asterisk mean?	_____
What does the first backslash indicate?	_____
What does the second backslash divide?	_____
What .EXE files are copied?	_____
What destination is assumed?	_____
Display the directory.	DIR/P
Copy the BASIC program files to the BASIC directory.	CD \BASIC COPY C:\DOS\BASIC*.*
Erase the BASIC files from your DOS directory.	ERASE \DOS\BASIC*.*
What is your default directory?	_____
In the above ERASE command, why is \DOS necessary?	_____

102   The DOS Book

Task	Procedure/Response
Copy the student files from the root directory of C: to your LETTERS subdirectory.	CD \WORD\LETTERS COPY C:\READ.ME COPY C:\SORTLIST COPY C:\DIR.FIL COPY C:*.TXT COPY C:\NOTICE.*
What two NOTICE files were copied?	_____
Copy the add-on utility programs and their documentation to your DOS directory.	COPY C:\LIST.COM \DOS COPY C:\SDIR.* \DOS COPY C:\FREE.* \DOS
What is the source location?	_____
What is the target location?	_____
Erase the files from the root of the C: drive.	ERASE C:\SDIR.* ERASE C:\READ.ME ERASE C:\NOTICE.* ERASE C:*.TXT ERASE C:\FREE.* ERASE C:\LIST.COM ERASE C:\SORTLIST ERASE C:\DIR.FIL
Make your \DOS directory the default.	CD\DOS
View the structure.	TREE/F
Where is the TREE.COM file?	_____
What additional information does /F show?	_____
What is the only file in the root?	_____
Send a copy of the TREE output to the printer.	TREE/F>PRN
Run the CHKDSK program.	CHKDSK

Task	Procedure/Response
How many bytes are free on your A: disk?	_____
How many directories have you made?	_____
How many user files are on your disk?	_____

The PATH Command

When a file is specified in any command, DOS looks for it in the current drive and directory. A path to any other directory can be specified with most DOS commands that take filenames. This path must be literally typed in with the command. Wildcards are not allowed. For example: Assume the default directory is WORD in our scheme considered earlier.

>TYPE \WORD\MEMOS\JONES\MEMO1

will start at the root, search for the file, move to the WORD directory, search there, and so on, until it finds the file or exhausts the path.

Although a path must be literally specified for DOS to find <u>text files</u> named in commands, DOS provides a way to set one permanent path which it will search automatically for command files (.COM or .EXE) or batch (.BAT) files. You used this application of PATH at the beginning of the course to set a path to the DOS commands in either the B or C drive. The PATH command allows the user to set such a default path. If no path is specified, DOS will look only in the current directory.

PATH \DOS;\BATCH	Instructs DOS to search the DOS and BATCH directories if the requested program is not in the current directory.
PATH	Displays the current path.
PATH;	Resets DOS to the default of searching only the current directory.

Activity 5-7: Setting and Using Paths

By setting a path to the \DOS directory on your student disk, you will be simulating the actual operation of a hard disk where both programs and files are stored on the same disk. You want to be able to access all DOS commands from any subdirectory on your disk.

* * *   We will no longer need to refer to the C: drive, since all the relevant DOS commands are on your student disk.   * * *

Task	Procedure/Response
Begin this activity in the root.	CD \
Try to run CHKDSK.	CHKDSK
Why is it a "Bad command or file name"?	_____
Set a new search path for .COM, .EXE and .BAT files.	PATH A:\;A:\DOS
Now try to check the disk structure.	CHKDSK/V
Why does it work now?	_____
Where has DOS found CHKDSK.COM?	_____
Change to the WORD directory and run CHKDSK.	CD \WORD CHKDSK/V
Display the contents of a file in the DOS directory.	TYPE \DOS\FREE.DOC
What is your default directory?	_____
Why can't you simply enter TYPE FREE.DOC, since \DOS is on the new path?	_____

The SUBST Command

SUBST (substitute) allows you to use a drive specifier to refer to another drive or path. If your application does not recognize paths, SUBST allows the use of a drive letter for a path.

SUBST D: A:\WORD\LETTERS   substitutes D: for path

TYPE D:MEMO.TXT   displays contents of file MEMO.TXT in the \WORD\LETTERS subdirectory.

The SUBSTitution remains in effect until you turn off the computer, or until you delete the substituted drive designator. To delete the above substitution, enter the command

    SUBST D: /d

The first D is the drive designator that was substituted for the \WORD\LETTERS path; the second d stands for delete.

On Your Own—Disk Organization

Task	Procedure	Response
Use your own name to make a personal directory which is a subdirectory of the root of A:.	_____	
Change into your own directory.	_____	
What is your prompt?		_____
Copy NOTICE and MEMO1.TXT from your \Word\Letters subdirectory into your own directory.	_____	
Remove NOTICE and MEMO1.TXT from the \Word\Letters subdirectory.	_____	
Create a two-line prompt that shows the current time on the first line and the current path and greater-than symbol on the second.	_____	
Return to the root directory.	_____	
What is your prompt?		_____
Print a TREE of all the directories and all the files on your student disk.	_____	

Summary—Disk Organization

1. Floppy-disk drives use both sides of the disk, 40 tracks per side, and 9 sectors per track for a total capacity of 368,640 bytes. Some of this is used for the directory and, if the system is transferred, another 40000-60000 bytes are used.

2. Disks must be formatted (FORMAT) before they can be used. The FORMAT/S option transfers the system to the new disk, making that disk bootable.

3. A tree structure for organizing files is provided by DOS. The top of the tree is called the root and all branches are called subdirectories.

4. Both internal (DIR, MD, CD, RD, PATH) and external commands (CHKDSK, TREE, BACKUP, RESTORE) are provided for managing the tree structure of subdirectories. The full file specification must be included for DOS to be able to find and execute external commands.

5. The PATH command allows you to set a path to command and batch files—that is, those with .COM, .EXE, or .BAT extensions—in any directory or to access a file in one directory from another by specifying its path.

6. The PROMPT command allows you to customize the DOS prompt; most useful is the PG prompt which presents the current path and the greater-than (>) symbol as the prompt.

Quick Check—Disk Organization

1. If a floppy disk can store about 360,000 bytes, a 20 megabyte (20 million bytes) hard disk has the same capacity as about

    a. 6 floppies.
    b. 60 floppies.
    c. 30 floppies.
    d. 20 floppies.

2. To be able to boot your system from the hard disk you must

    a. partition the entire hard disk for DOS.
    b. never format the hard disk.
    c. create a volume label for the hard disk.
    d. format the hard disk with the FORMAT/S command.

3. The ROOT directory

    a. is the default directory when DOS is booted.
    b. can contain only .COM files.
    c. must be the last directory created in a tree structure.
    d. is designated with the symbol /.

4. DOS provides subdirectory capability to

    a. make it harder for someone to find and possibly destroy your files.
    b. allow the great number of files possible on a hard disk to be stored in an organized fashion.
    c. make floppy disks act like hard disks.
    d. allow a greater amount of data to be stored on a disk.

5. The TREE command

    a. displays the contents of the root directory only.
    b. cannot be used in versions of DOS earlier than 3.1.
    c. displays all the subdirectories at all levels on the specified drive.
    d. has no option for showing filenames in subdirectories.

6. To change from one first-level directory to another first-level directory,

    a. you must switch disks.
    b. just type the name of the new directory.
    c. enter the command CD <directory name>.
    d. enter the command CD \<directory name>.

7. The best way to keep track of which directory is the current default is to

   a. change the prompt to show the default directory.
   b. type HELP.
   c. type CD.
   d. always return to the root directory.

8. To TYPE a text file in the Jones subdirectory of the Memos subdirectory of the Word subdirectory, enter the command

   a. TYPE <file name>\Jones\Memos\Word.

   b. TYPE /Word/Memos/Jones/<file name>.

   c. TYPE \Word\Memos\Jones\<file name>.

   d. TYPE \Word\Memos\Jones <file name>.

9. Copying files into appropriate subdirectories
   (more than one correct answer possible)

   a. can be accomplished by changing into the source directory and defining the full path address of the destination directory.
   b. can be accomplished by changing into the destination directory and defining the full path address of the source directory.
   c. can be accomplished from any subdirectory by defining the full path address of both the source and the destination directory.
   d. can only be accomplished from the root directory.

10. The PATH command

    a. allows any file to be accessed from any subdirectory.
    b. instructs DOS to search through all the subdirectories listed in the path to find the requested file.
    c. can be used only to display the currently set path.
    d. instructs DOS to search through all the listed subdirectories for command (.COM or .EXE) files or batch (.BAT) files.

UNIT·6·

Creating DOS Files

Overview: You can use DOS to create text files in one of two ways: using the COPY CON (console) command or the EDLIN line editor. The activities in this section use COPY and EDLIN to create simple text files.

Topics: Creating files with COPY CON

Editing files with EDLIN

Creating files with EDLIN

The COPY Command Revisited

The COPY command has many features. You have already used it to backup files on the same or a different disk and to move files between subdirectories. COPY can also be use to copy input from the keyboard (console or CON—a DOS device name, as is PRN) to a file. In the following activity you will create a simple text file, HELLO.TXT, using COPY.

The COPY command has two parts: the source (what you are copying FROM) and the destination, or target (what you are copying TO). In the COPY CON <FILENAME> command, the source is CON—that is, you are creating a source document at the keyboard. You instruct DOS that the source is complete by pressing the [F6] key and then [RETURN]. This places the symbol ^Z (Control-Z) on the screen. This is the DOS end-of-file marker. When the source is complete, DOS executes the command—copying the source to the destination; in this case the target file is created.

Activity 6-1: Using COPY to Create a DOS File

In this activity you will create a simple text file. If you make a typing error while entering the text before pressing return, just use the [Left Arrow] or [Backspace] to erase. If you made an error and already pressed return, you cannot change it from within the COPY command; therefore, just continue entering the rest of the text.

Task	Procedure/Response
Begin this activity in the root directory.	CD \
Create a simple text file named HELLO.TXT using COPY.	COPY CON HELLO.TXT
What is the source?	_____
What is the destination?	_____
When the cursor appears at the left edge of the screen, enter the text, pressing [Return] at the end of <u>each</u> line.	HELLO! Welcome to _____'s PC (put your name in the blank) This is Version 1 Bye.
Can you use the [Up Arrow] key to return to a previous line?	_____
Complete the source document and execute the copy command.	[F6] <u>and</u> [Return]
Get a directory to check whether your new file is included.	DIR
When was it created?	_____
How large is it?	_____
List the file to the screen.	TYPE HELLO.TXT
How would you list the file to the printer?	_____

File Creation and Editing Using EDLIN

EDLIN is a DOS external program (EDLIN.COM). It must reside in the default directory or be contained in a directory on the PATH so that DOS can find it and load it into RAM. It is executed with a two-word command: EDLIN <filename>. If the file to be edited is not in the current directory, its full path must be designated.

EDLIN is a simple line editor that allows you to create and edit DOS files and programs. EDLIN is line oriented rather than screen oriented like most word-processing programs. This means that lines are numbered and edited one line at a time by number. Each line can have up to 253 characters. There are 14 subcommands in EDLIN. These are:

APPEND	(A)	adds text to end of file
COPY	(C)	copies lines to another location
DELETE	(D)	deletes line
EDIT		enter line number to edit line
END EDIT	(E)	exits EDLIN and saves file
INSERT	(I)	enters insert mode (use [Ctrl][C] to exit Insert Mode)
LIST	(L)	displays lines of text on screen
QUIT	(Q)	exits EDLIN without saving file
MOVE	(M)	moves text within file
PAGE	(P)	displays lines after current line
REPLACE	(R)	replaces specified text
SEARCH	(S)	searches for specified text
TRANSFER	(T)	transfers text from an outside file
WRITE	(W)	writes specified lines to a new file

Lines are numbered automatically by EDLIN, and all commands operate on a line or range of lines that are specified before the subcommand. EDLIN commands can be entered in upper- or lowercase at the EDLIN prompt, an asterisk (*). Following the conventions observed throughout this course, all EDLIN commands are shown in UPPER case. You must press [Return] after every command or line of text entered into EDLIN. Many of the commands are illustrated in the activities that follow.

Use of Function Keys and Editing Keys with EDLIN

The function keys [F1] through [F4] are quite useful when editing text files with EDLIN. Indeed, these keys can be used in like manner when entering DOS commands. When a line is entered into EDLIN (or when a DOS command is entered at the DOS prompt) that line is stored as a template in RAM. That template, or parts of it, can be replayed using the function keys as follows:

[F1] Replays one character at a time from the template
 [NOTE: The right arrow key has the same effect.]

[F2] Replays all characters from the template UP TO, but not including, the first occurrence of the next key typed after [F2] is pressed.

 Example: COPY *.TXT A: (this line is stored as template)

 [F2] T—replays COPY *. (all characters up to T.)

[F3] Replays all remaining characters from the template. If the cursor is at the beginning, all characters will be repeated.

[F4] Skips over all characters up to the first occurrence of the next key typed after [F4] is pressed. (This is the opposite of [F2].)

[INS] Allows insertion of characters into the template at the cursor position. The [INS] key must be pressed for each line into which characters are to be inserted.

[DEL] Deletes (erases) from the template the character at the cursor position.

[ESC] Cancels the line currently being displayed. The template remains unchanged.

Activity 6-2: Using EDLIN to Edit HELLO.TXT

Task	Procedure/Response
Use Edlin to edit HELLO.TXT.	EDLIN HELLO.TXT
Where is the file EDLIN.COM?	_____
How does DOS find it if your default is the root?	_____
What message does EDLIN display when the file to be edited has been loaded into RAM?	_____
What is the EDLIN prompt?	_____
List the file.	L
Change line 3 to version 2. Display the line up to the # 1.	3 [F2] 1
Enter a 2.	2
List the file again.	L
Insert two new lines beginning at line 4.	4I EDLIN is a useful program <your text here>
REMINDER: Press [Return] after <u>each</u> line.	
Exit Insert Mode.	[Ctrl] [C]
List the file.	L
How many lines does it contain?	_____
Edit line 4 inserting "very" before useful.	4 [F2] u [INS] very [space]

Task	Procedure/Response
Complete the line.	[F3]
List the file.	L
Delete lines 4 to 6.	4,6D
List the file.	L
Exit EDLIN and save the edited file.	E
Find the new file in the directory.	DIR
View the file.	TYPE HELLO.TXT

Note: HELLO.BAK is a backup file. What do you think it contains? How can you find out?

Activity 6-3: Creating A File with EDLIN

EDLIN can be used to create files as well as edit files created with COPY CON. A new file name is given in the EDLIN <filename> command. (That file will be stored in the current directory, unless a full path address directs it to another directory.) The message "New file" appears before the EDLIN prompt. The command to enter Insert Mode (I) allows new lines to be created beginning with line 1. The [CTRL] [C] command exits Insert Mode when you are finished entering new lines.

Task	Procedure/Response
Execute EDLIN to create a new file.	EDLIN \WORD\MEMOS\SMITH\MYNOTE
What is your default directory?	_____
Where will the new file be stored?	_____
What is the new file's name?	_____
What message does EDLIN display when you are not using it to edit an existing file?	_____
Enter Insert Mode.	I
Compose a four- or five-line message. Remember to press [Return] at the end of each line.	
Exit Insert Mode.	[Ctrl] [C]
View your message.	L
Make any necessary corrections.	
Exit EDLIN.	E
Print your message.	TYPE \WORD\MEMOS\SMITH\MYNOTE>PRN

On Your Own — Creating DOS Files

Task	Procedure	Response
Use the SUBST command to make it easier to indicate the location of MYNOTE. Create the new drive F:	_____	
View a directory of your new drive.	_____	
How many files does it contain?		_____
EDLIN MYNOTE (remember to tell DOS where to find MYNOTE). Add a few more lines. Print the new version.	_____	
Create a short note with COPY CON (call it MYNOTE2) in the root directory. Tell a friend of your plans for the weekend.	_____	
Print MYNOTE2.	_____	

Challenge:

Task	Procedure	Response
Use the computer as a typewriter. Create letter to your grandmother (or someone else) that is created at the console and printed but never saved in a file.	_____	
What is the source?		_____
What is the destination?		_____

Summary — Creating DOS Files

1. DOS files can be created using the COPY CON command, the EDLIN line editor, or a word processing program.

2. COPY allows no editing once a line has been entered but is the fastest way to create short files, since it is an internal command.

3. EDLIN is a limited line editor with 14 subcommands. It can be used to edit existing DOS-readable files or create new ones.

Quick Check — Creating DOS Files

1. How do you create a file named FILE8.MY using COPY?

2. What is the difference between a line editor and a screen editor?

3. How do you tell DOS you are through entering text with COPY CON?

4. What is the advantage and disadvantage of COPY rather than EDLIN?

UNIT·7·

Batch Files

Overview: When you find yourself entering the same sequence of commands repeatedly, you are ready to create batch files. In this unit you will create both simple and sophisticated batch files that will greatly enhance your computer's efficiency.

Topics: Batch file names

Comparison of batch files and text files

Batch file commands

Batch file variables

AUTOEXEC.BAT

Batch Files

A <u>batch file</u> is a sequence of operations that acts together (as a "batch") to perform some routine task. A batch file can be thought of as a DOS program that can be called at any point in a computer operation, including as part of another program or file. Batch files are used to automate a series of commands or procedures that are repeated on a regular basis without user intervention or interaction.

Batch files in DOS consist of executable commands in sequential order. All the DOS commands considered thus far could be contained in batch files. DOS provides simple variable facilities for passing values to a batch file at the time of execution (run time), and rudimentary looping and branching control structures. This has the effect of providing a simple programming language for batch files. All DOS batch files must have the extension ".BAT".

Sample batch file names:

   PROG.BAT

   MENU1.BAT

   1.BAT

   INSTALL.BAT

Similarities/Differences Between Batch Files and Text Files

How They Are Alike

Both batch files and text files are:

- Created with COPY CON or EDLIN.

- Edited with EDLIN.

- Viewed using the TYPE command.

- Can display information to the screen.

How They Are Different

- Text files <u>require</u> no extension, although the .TXT extension is commonly used.

- Batch files <u>must</u> contain the .BAT extension.

- Batch files can be executed by entering their name minus the .BAT extension.

- Text files can only be viewed; they perform no action but simply display a message on the screen when called with the TYPE command.

- Batch files can be run from a subdirectory that is on the default path; text files must be referenced from within the subdirectory in which they are stored or must have a full pathname, for example, TYPE \WORD\JONES\MEMO\NEWMEMO.TXT.

126   The DOS Book

Activity 7-1: Creating A Batch File to Display the Contents of A File and Change Directories

The premise: Your secretary is unfamiliar with DOS. He/she uses the computer only for word processing. You have structured your hard disk so that the word-processing program and the data files your secretary uses are in the WORD directory. You want to leave daily instructions on the computer, then change to the WORD directory for your secretary.

This batch file, called HELLO.BAT, displays on the screen the contents of a message file, then changes to the appropriate directory.

Task	Procedure/Response
Begin this activity in the BATCH directory of A:.	CD \BATCH
Use EDLIN to create the batch file named HELLO.BAT.	EDLIN HELLO.BAT
In which directory will this file be saved?	_____
Enter Insert mode.	I
Enter the program lines.	CLS TYPE \HELLO.TXT CLS CD \WORD
Exit Insert mode.	[Ctrl][C]
Exit EDLIN, saving the file.	E
Place the BATCH directory on the path, so this file can be executed from within any directory.	PATH A:\;A:\DOS;A:\BATCH
Test the batch file.	HELLO
Which subdirectory are you in after executing HELLO.BAT?	_____

Task	Procedure/Response

HELLO.BAT could use some refinement to make it more "user-friendly." The user doesn't need to see all the commands echoed to the screen, and he/she certainly doesn't have time to read the message as it zooms by.

Task	Procedure/Response
Edit the file HELLO.BAT.	EDLIN \BATCH\HELLO.BAT
Why did you need to include \BATCH?	_____
List the file.	L
Suppress DOS's echoing commands to the screen.	1I ECHO OFF [Ctrl][C]

REMINDER: After adding or deleting lines, line numbers may change. Always list the file after inserting or deleting.

Task	Procedure/Response
List the file.	L
Allow time for reading the text.	4I PAUSE [Ctrl][C]
List the file.	L
Add a remark to identify the file. (Type this on one line.)	3I REM This is my secretary's daily start-up file. [Ctrl][C]
List the file.	L
Insert blank lines between the text message and the pause message. In DOS versions 3.0 and above, spaces in batch files are represented by the ASCII character 255 (typed from the numeric keypad).	5I ECHO [Alt]255 ECHO [Alt]255 ECHO [Alt]255 [Ctrl][C]

Task	Procedure/Response
List the file.	L
Exit EDLIN, saving the file.	E
Test the batch file.	HELLO
What message does PAUSE display?	_____
To leave a different message, which file would you edit?	_____

Activity 7-2: Creating A Simple Batch File to Prevent Accidental Formatting of A Hard Disk

All data, programs, files, and so on, stored on your hard disk will be lost if the disk is ever accidentally reformatted. There is no failsafe feature in the FORMAT program that asks you whether you really want to format your hard disk. Therefore, hard disk managers must be responsible for making sure this doesn't happen.

Task	Procedure/Response
Rename the FORMAT program so anyone typing "FORMAT" will be requesting FORMAT.BAT not FORMAT.COM.	RENAME \DOS\FORMAT.COM TAMROF.COM
Does changing a file name alter its contents?	_____
What command would you type to run the renamed FORMAT program?	_____
Use EDLIN to create the file in the BATCH directory.	CD \ BATCH EDLIN FORMAT.BAT
Enter Insert mode.	I
Enter the program lines.	ECHO OFF REM Simple format protection CLS TAMROF A: CLS
Exit Insert mode.	[Ctrl] [C]
Exit EDLIN, saving the file.	E
Display the file.	TYPE FORMAT.BAT
Where is the actual command to perform the formatting?	_____

Task	Procedure/Response

What disk will ALWAYS be formatted using this method? _____

CAUTION: Before you test this program, remember you are requesting to format the disk in the A drive, <u>your student files disk</u>. You will be prompted to insert the disk you wish to format in the A drive. Replace your student disk with a blank disk before hitting a key . . . or press [CTRL] [C]. Please don't format your student files disk.

Task	Procedure/Response
Test the program carefully.	FORMAT C: (Attempt to format the hard disk)

Batch File Variables

DOS allows use of ten variables in batch files. The variable names are %0, %1, %2, ... %9. The %0 is automatically assigned the value of the default drive and the batch file containing it.

Using variables in a batch file allows DOS to replace the variables with actual values when the batch file executes. The user enters the values for any variables when the batch file is called for execution.

Example:

Suppose a batch file named T.BAT contained the following line:

>   TYPE %1>PRN

The user would call the program by typing the name of the batch file followed by a space and the name of the file to be copied to the printer, that is

>   T HELLO1.TXT

Note that the .BAT extension is not typed. This command would send a copy of the file HELLO1.TXT to the printer. In effect this batch file allows the user to abbreviate the TYPE command as T and automatically redirects the output to the printer.

Exiting from a Batch File

A running batch file will execute each command in turn, one after the other, until it reaches the end of its commands. If you want to stop the batch file before it has processed all the commands, type [Ctrl][C]. The message: "Terminate batch job (Y/N)?" will appear. Press Y to stop processing and return to the DOS prompt. Pressing N only ends the command that was executing when [Ctrl][C] was pressed; processing resumes with the next command in the batch file.

As a batch file executes, DOS "remembers" what batch file it is running. A batch file can, as we will see later, call an application program. You may, while running the application program, need to remove the disk containing your batch file, perhaps to insert a data disk. When you exit from the application program, DOS "remembers" it was running a batch file and will try to return to the batch file to complete its execution. If that file is no longer available, the message: "Insert disk with batch file and strike any key when ready" will appear. The batch processor will execute the next command in the file when that file is on the disk in the appropriate drive.

Activity 7-3: Creating A More Sophisticated Batch File to Prevent Accidental Formatting of A Hard Disk

An experienced computer user would be able to circumvent even this level of protection, but hopefully he/she would know better than to reformat a hard disk without backing up all files and data.

* * * **Before beginning this activity, you must copy and rename the files used in Activity 7-2 if you want to preserve them for future use.** * * *

    (1) COPY \DOS\TAMROF.COM to \DOS\PREVENT

Without the .COM extension this file (PREVENT) is not executable.

    (2) RENAME FORMAT.BAT to FORMAT1.BAT

Task	Procedure/Response
Use EDLIN to create this file in the BATCH directory.	EDLIN FORMAT.BAT
Get into insert mode.	I
Enter the program lines.	ECHO OFF REM MAXIMUM FORMAT PROTECTION CLS IF %1==a: GOTO OK IF %1==A: GOTO OK ECHO THIS PROGRAM ONLY FORMATS ECHO FLOPPY DISKS IN THE A:DRIVE GOTO END :OK RENAME \PREVENT PREVENT.COM PREVENT A: %2 %3 RENAME \PREVENT.COM PREVENT :END

Task	Procedure/Response
What was the original name of PREVENT.COM?	_____
Exit insert mode.	[Ctrl][C]
List the file and edit as necessary.	L
Exit EDLIN, save file.	E

* * * * *

When a user enters FORMAT, he/she will get your batch file instead of the FORMAT.COM file. If the format request is for the A: drive, the program will rename PREVENT to an executable file, execute it, and rename it to a nonexecuting file. If the request is for the C: drive, the user will be given your message and returned to the prompt.

Test the program carefully.	FORMAT C: {attempt to format the hard drive}
	FORMAT A:

CAUTION: If you decide to test the program, replace your student disk with a blank floppy disk before pressing [Return]. The [Ctrl][C] command will abort a batch file.

Activity 7-3: Annotation

Program Line	Annotation
ECHO OFF	Suppresses DOS's echoing of commands to the screen.
REM MAXIMUM FORMAT PROTECTION	Inserts a remark in the file to identify it. With ECHO OFF, this remark is not visible on the screen.
CLS	Clears the screen.
IF %1==a: GOTO OK	Allows conditional execution of commands, depending upon the characters entered when the batch file was called. The file would be executed at the DOS prompt by typing FORMAT. The batch file name always corresponds to variable %0. The next character string typed (following a space, which separates one character string from another) is variable %1. The double equal symbol (==) establishes a character string identity—that is, if the first variable is identical to "a:".
	If this condition is met—if "FORMAT a:" was typed— the batch commands will continue executing following the line containing the appropriate label—OK. A label is inserted into a batch file as a colon [:] followed by the label name. Any commands between the IF command and the line following the :OK label will be ignored if FORMAT a: was typed.
IF %1==A: GOTO OK	If the first condition was not met ("FORMAT a:" was not typed), this second condition will be tested for. This allows the user to enter either an upper- or lowercase A with the same result.

Program Line	Annotation
ECHO .... GOTO END	If neither of the two acceptable conditions are met—if anything other than FORMAT a: or FORMAT A: was typed—the commands between the GOTO OK and the :OK LABEL are not skipped, the messages following the ECHO command will be displayed, and the batch commands will continue executing following the :END label, which would return the DOS prompt.
:OK	Label indicating the line AFTER WHICH batch file execution will continue following the GOTO OK command.
RENAME \PREVENT PREVENT.COM	Previous to running FORMAT.BAT, FORMAT.COM was renamed PREVENT. There is no .COM extension, so PREVENT is a nonexecutable file. If everything is OK (if FORMAT A: or a: was typed), PREVENT will be renamed PREVENT.COM and will now be executable by typing PREVENT at the DOS prompt.
PREVENT A: %2 %3	The original DOS FORMAT program will be executed to format the disk in drive A:. If "FORMAT A: /S" or "FORMAT A: /V" or "FORMAT A: /S /V" was typed, the S and V parameters will be substituted for the %2 and %3 variables and the newly formatted disk will be bootable and/or have a volume name.
RENAME \PREVENT.COM PREVENT	When the formatting procedure is finished, the executable file is renamed to PREVENT making it no longer executable (typing PREVENT at the DOS prompt will return the message: "Bad command or file name").
:END	Label indicating the line AFTER WHICH batch file execution will continue following the GOTO END command.

AUTOEXEC.BAT

When DOS is booted, it looks for a special batch file named AUTOEXEC.BAT. If it finds this file, it executes it immediately after completing the booting operation. This provides a way to automatically load or execute programs upon powering up the system.

Since DOS looks for AUTOEXEC.BAT upon booting, this file must reside on a floppy disk which has the DOS system commands (COMMAND.COM and the hidden files, IBMBIO.COM and IBMDOS.COM) on it or in the root directory of the hard disk.

An AUTOEXEC.BAT file can accomplish routine housekeeping and setup tasks, in addition to loading application programs and changing directories. Some commands commonly found in AUTOEXEC.BAT files are:

DATE   Automatic date and time prompts are not displayed when an AUTOEXEC.BAT file exists.

TIME

PATH   Establishes the directories in which DOS is to look for commands and executable files not found in the root directory.

CD   Change from root to designated directory.

PROMPT   This command allows you to customize the DOS prompt. When used with the options PG, the prompt will display the current directory.

WP
LOTUS
DBASE   Loads and runs application program or .BAT file.
MENU

Activity 7-4: Creating and Using an AUTOEXEC.BAT File

This activity creates a representative AUTOEXEC.BAT file. You can customize it for your particular system and configuration.

Task	Procedure/Response
Begin this activity in the root.	CD \
Use EDLIN to create the file.	EDLIN AUTOEXEC.BAT
Get into insert mode.	I
Enter the program lines.	ECHO OFF REM AUTOEXEC FILE DATE TIME CLS PATH A:\;A:\DOS;A:\BATCH PROMPT PG ECHO WELCOME BACK PAUSE HELLO
What file will be executed by the line HELLO?	_____
Exit insert mode.	[Ctrl][C]
Exit EDLIN, Save file.	E
Test the AUTOEXEC.BAT file.	AUTOEXEC or [Ctrl][Alt][Del]
Should this file be transferred to the BATCH directory?	_____
Why or why not?	_____

On Your Own—Batch Files

Task	Procedure	Response
Change to your \BATCH directory.	_____	
Create a batch file called D that will display a directory of the disk in drive A:.		
What extension must your file have?		_____
Modify D.BAT so DOS commands are not ECHOed to the screen and the directory displays on a clear screen.		
Modify D.BAT so it can be used to display a directory of any disk the user requests.		
Use D.BAT to see a directory of the hard disk.	_____	
Modify your AUTOEXEC.BAT to insert three blank lines between the message "Welcome Back" and the message produced by PAUSE.		

Summary—Batch Files

1. Batch files allow you to automate routine tasks. They contain a series of executable DOS commands (that could be entered interactively from the keyboard) that are executed one after another automatically by entering only the name of the batch file.

2. Batch files can be created using COPY CON, EDLIN, or a word processor. They must follow DOS file-naming rules, and must have .BAT as their extension. Batch files are executed by typing their name at the DOS prompt.

3. DOS provides special batch-processing subcommands that are not regular executable DOS commands. They are used to control the flow of the batch file from one command to another.

4. In batch files, DOS allows the use of variables, or dummy parameters, that are replaced by values supplied when the batch file executes. The batch file name itself is always variable %0. Variables are separated by spaces and the replacement values are also separated by spaces.

5. Long messages are often displayed as part of batch files by including a command to TYPE a .TXT file. Shorter messages can be displayed using the ECHO subcommand.

6. Batch files are often used to automate certain disk- management procedures (such as changing directories) for computer users not familiar with DOS. They are also used to control access to certain DOS commands (such as FORMAT).

7. AUTOEXEC.BAT is a special batch file which DOS looks for immediately after booting. If such a file is in the root directory of the default drive, control is passed to it immediately. AUTOEXEC.BAT files often contain such basic system set-up procedures as setting the path and customizing the DOS prompt.

Quick Check—Batch Files

Each question may have more than one correct answer.

1. Batch files can consist of

    a. any executable DOS command.
    b. special batch file subcommands.
    c. variables.
    d. commands to run other batch files.

2. Batch files are useful

    a. only to programmers, since they are actually small programs.
    b. to automate frequently repeated sequences of commands.
    c. to make computer access easier to novice computer users.
    d. only with hard disk systems.

3. Batch file names

    a. may contain variables.
    b. are typed to execute a batch file.
    c. can contain up to eight characters and any up-to-three character extension.
    d. must be typed in all capital letters.

4. Batch files can be created

    a. using COPY CON.
    b. using EDLIN.
    c. using a word processor.
    d. only in versions of DOS above 3.0.

5. The PAUSE subcommand

    a. is very useful after a TYPE command in a batch file.
    b. can be used only once per batch file.
    c. produces the message "Strike any key to continue" at the time of batch execution.
    d. has no effect if ECHO is OFF.

6. The GOTO subcommand

    a. can be used only with the IF subcommand.
    b. must be used in conjunction with a label name.
    c. must have a colon [:] before it.
    d. causes commands to be executed immediately before the label.

7. The ECHO subcommand
    a. has no effect once ECHO OFF or ECHO ON has been used.
    b. can be used to display messages on the screen during a batch file execution.
    c. is the best way to display long messages in batch files.
    d. overrides ECHO OFF by displaying any text which follows it, regardless of the status of ECHO OFF or ECHO ON.

8. Restricting access to certain commands (such as FORMAT) through batch processing
    a. is a good way to protect against accidental use of the wrong command.
    b. is a good way to protect against malicious "sabotage" by people who know their way around computers.
    c. often involves renaming DOS commands.
    d. often involves creating a batch file with the same name as the original command.

9. To interrupt a batch file before it has finished processing each of its commands
    a. is very dangerous.
    b. can be accomplished by typing [Ctrl][C].
    c. can be accomplished by pressing [Esc].
    d. is best accomplished by turning off the computer.

10. AUTOEXEC.BAT is a special file that
    a. must reside in the root directory of the boot disk.
    b. can be used to set system defaults so that they don't have to be reset by the user each time the machine is booted.
    c. cannot be used to automatically load an application.
    c. can be called AUTOMATE.BAT, if you prefer.

UNIT·8·

Creating a Menu System

Overview: Computer systems are becoming increasingly easy for people to use. A primary driving force for this trend is the need for noncomputer specialists to use computers on a routine basis. Computer specialists learn to deal with the cumbersome messages and mannerisms of computers because it is their job to do so. People who use computers as tools in their regular work do not have the time or inclination to adapt themselves to the computer, so system designers must adapt the computer system to them. Many factors have contributed to this trend: more powerful hardware, improved software tools, and especially increased attention and experience to the human interface on the part of system designers and programmers. Everyone wants to sell or use "user-friendly" systems.

Topics: Command vs. Menu-Driven Systems

Considering Menu Design

Mapping a Directory Structure

Creating the MENU.TXT File

Creating the MENU.BAT File

Creating the Menu-Selection Batch Files

Automating the System

Command and Menu-Driven Systems

Command-driven systems

One technique for making systems easy to use is to make the commands for using a system intrinsically meaningful, for example, TYPE is a better way to command the machine to display (type) a file than O4567, OP, or even T. Systems that are controlled through commands are called command-driven systems. Experts prefer command-driven systems since they can complete tasks quickly and efficiently by using terse commands which they have memorized through much practice. Casual users, and certainly novice users, often have difficulty with command-driven systems (even with those that have intrinsically meaningful commands) because they must constantly refer to a list of commands to accomplish tasks.

Menu-driven systems

A second, very popular way to make systems easy to use is to provide menus for users. A menu-driven system allows the user to accomplish routine tasks by choosing from a set of options explicitly displayed on the screen, that is, by selecting from a menu of choices. Menu systems allow nonexperts to use systems to perform previously defined tasks without knowing the system commands to initiate those tasks.

Menu-driven systems have two disadvantages. They limit flexibility and user control, since all tasks the system performs must be previously defined and incorporated as choices in the menu. Secondly, menu systems slow down expert users, since they must move through screens of menus to accomplish straightforward tasks. Many systems are now both menu driven and command driven. In these systems, menus are displayed, but users can enter commands directly or choose from the menu. Lotus 1-2-3 was one of the first microcomputer packages to offer this type of user interface, and this feature certainly contributed to its popularity and success. New approaches to the user interface include the use of graphic (iconic) menus and commands, as in the Apple MacIntosh computer.

Menu Characteristics

A well-designed menu should be:

Easy to read—

>words should be chosen carefully, avoid jargon.
>screen should be uncluttered.
>complex sets of choices should be broken into separate screens.
>spacing, character size, and screen intensity should be appropriate.

Easy to use—

>choices should be clearly articulated.
>minimal keystrokes or physical movements should be required for any choice.
>escapes should be built in.
>clear indications of current levels help avoid "menu floundering".

Aesthetically pleasing—

>eye pleasing screens encourage use.
>symmetry helps.

Steps in Menu Creation

In this unit you will create a simple menu system. Creating a menu system includes three major components: planning the menu, implementing it on the system, and testing it.

For the purpose of this unit, assume you have a system which is used for database management, spreadsheets, and word processing. You wish to easily choose one of these options after turning the power on. When exiting from one of these packages the menu should be displayed again. An option to exit from the menu system is also required. You will complete the following steps to implement and test a menu system for this situation.

1. Map a tree structure of the directory for the various applications programs, batch files, and data files.

2. Create a text file to serve as the menu, and a batch file to call the text file.

3. Create a batch file for each choice in the menu.

4. Modify AUTOEXEC.BAT to display the menu upon booting the system.

5. Test and debug the system.

Mapping a Directory (Tree) Structure

The menu system will allow the user to move easily through the programs and files organized in the structure depicted below.
Directories are displayed with their files. In using your simulated hard disk, you will load actual programs from their respective directories on drive C:, since they were not copied to your A: disk.

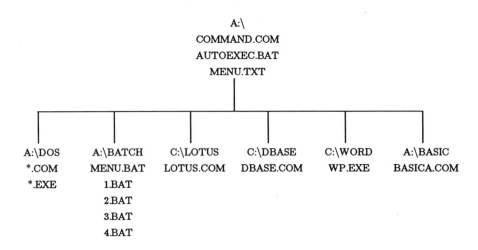

Figure 8-1

NOTE: If LOTUS, dBASE, and/or WordPerfect are not available on the hard disk, but other similar programs are available, substitute directory and program names.

If no application programs are available on the hard disk, substitute the similarly named directories from the A: drive. Rather than loading actual programs, the students will TYPE text files stored in A:\LOTUS, A:\DBASE, A:\WORD to simulate the loading of the respective programs. See Activity 8-3.

The steps in the following activity will display a menu that looks like this:

```
┌─────────────────────┐
│     MAIN MENU       │
└─────────────────────┘
```

Type the number of your choice and press [Return].

<1> Lotus 1-2-3—A powerful spreadsheet package.

<2> dBASE III—A relational database management system.

<3> WordPerfect—A comprehensive word processor program.

<4> EXIT to DOS—To do tasks not included above.

Using Extended-Character Set Graphics

IBM-compatible monitors can display graphic characters entered by using their Extended-Character Set numeric code. These codes are entered by holding down the [Alt] key, typing the three-digit number using the numeric keypad (NOT the row of numerals across the top of the keyboard), then releasing the [Alt] key. Codes for graphic characters useful in drawing boxes on the screen are presented below.

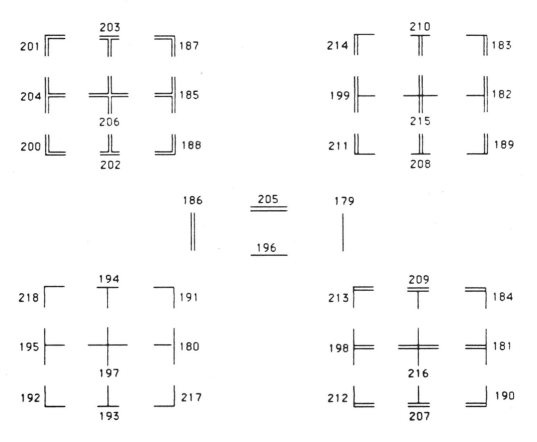

Figure 8-3

Activity 8-1: Creating the Menu Text File

Task	Procedure
Change to root directory.	CD \
Use EDLIN to create MENU.TXT.	EDLIN MENU.TXT
Get into insert mode.	I
Enter text. The screen uses 25 lines, your menu should be about 20 lines long, leaving some room at the bottom for user input. Enter the lines as they appear in Figure 8-3.	Enter the lines
To force a blank line to be displayed, just enter a Return while in EDLIN.	
To position lines horizontally, type spaces.	
Exit insert, proof your file, save and exit EDLIN.	[Ctrl][C] L E
Test the menu for format.	CLS TYPE MENU.TXT
If necessary, improve the format by getting back into EDLIN and editing lines.	
Inserting spaces will "walk" lines to the right across the screen. Deleting spaces will move lines to the left.	

Activity 8-2: Creating the Batch File that Calls MENU.TXT

This batch file will call the MENU.TXT file, thus displaying the menu. It will then change the directory to BATCH so the batch files corresponding to each choice are available.

Task	Procedure/Response
Begin this activity in the BATCH directory.	CD \BATCH
Use EDLIN to create MENU.BAT.	EDLIN MENU.BAT
Get into input mode.	I
Enter lines.	ECHO OFF REM Calls MENU.TXT CLS TYPE A:\MENU.TXT
Why is the full path address for MENU.TXT necessary?	_____
Exit insert mode.	Press [Ctrl][C]
Exit EDLIN, Save file.	E
Test the batch file.	MENU

If the batch file is working properly, the menu will be displayed.

Activity 8-3: Creating Batch Files to Change Directories and Load Applications

You will create a batch file for each of the five choices on the menu. Each batch file will clear the screen, change to the proper directory, and load the requested application. After the application is exited, the menu is displayed again, except for the case where the user chooses DOS. In that case the batch file terminates.

If application programs are not available on the hard disk, go to Activity 8-3: For Systems without Available Application Program.

Task	Procedure/Response
Begin this activity in the BATCH directory.	CD \BATCH
Create 1.BAT, the file called if the user selects choice 1, Lotus 1-2-3.	EDLIN 1.BAT
You will not be told to enter insert mode or to exit from EDLIN and save the file for the remainder of this activity.	
Enter the lines.	ECHO OFF REM Calls Lotus 1-2-3 CLS
[Change default to hard disk]	C: CD \LOTUS (or name of LOTUS directory)
[Load application] [Return default to A: drive] [Execute MENU.BAT]	LOTUS A: MENU
Test the file.	1

What does the "1" represent? _____

NOTE: To exit LOTUS, type E.

Task	Procedure/Response

Task **Procedure/Response**

<u>On Your Own</u>

Create 2.BAT to load dBASE and 3BAT to load WordPerfect.

Create 4.BAT   EDLIN 4.BAT

Enter lines.   ECHO OFF
                                                 REM Exit to DOS
                                                 CLS
                                                 CD \
                                                 REM Do not return to Menu

Test the batch files.

To EXIT from the application programs:

    LOTUS—Type E

    dBASE—Type QUIT [Return]

    WordPerfect—Press [F7]
                Type N
                      Y

Use EDLIN to correct any errors.

Activity 8-3: For Systems Without Available Application Programs

Part 1: CREATING TEST FILES IN EACH DIRECTORY

Rather than actually loading application programs, your menu system batch files will change to appropriate directories on your A: disk (where applications would be stored if they were available), TYPE an appropriate text file, then redisplay the menu.

Use EDLIN to create test files for each directory.

Task	Procedure/Response
Change to A:\LOTUS.	CD \LOTUS
Use EDLIN to create TEST.LOT.	EDLIN TEST.LOT
Enter Insert Mode.	I
Enter file lines.	You have found the Lotus Directory. If LOTUS.COM were available, it would be executing. CONGRATULATIONS!
Exit Insert Mode.	[Ctrl] [C]
Exit EDLIN.	E

On Your Own

Repeat the above steps for TEST.DBS and TEST.WP creating each in its own directory. Be sure to substitute the appropriate program names for LOTUS in the text file.

Part 2: CREATING BATCH FILES TO CHANGE DIRECTORIES

Task	Procedure/Response
Begin this activity in the BATCH directory.	CD \BATCH
Create 1.BAT, the file called if the user selects choice 1, Lotus 1-2-3.	EDLIN 1.BAT
Enter Insert Mode.	I
Enter the lines.	ECHO OFF REM Calls Lotus Test File CLS CD \LOTUS TYPE TEST.LOT PAUSE MENU
Exit EDLIN.	E

On Your Own

Repeat the above steps for 2.BAT and 3.BAT to type TEST.DBS and TEST.WP. Remember to first change to the relevant directory.

Create 4.BAT	EDLIN 4.BAT
Enter lines.	ECHO OFF REM Exit to DOS CLS CD \ REM Do not return to Menu

Activity 8-4: Automating the Menu System

Task	Procedure/Response
Clear the screen.	CLS or 4 from the menu.
Change to the root directory.	CD \
Use EDLIN to modify AUTOEXEC.BAT.	EDLIN AUTOEXEC.BAT
Edit the last line to call MENU.BAT rather than HELLO.BAT.	13 [Return] MENU [Return]
What would you now expect to happen upon booting up from the disk in drive A:?	_____
List the file.	L
Exit EDLIN.	E
Test the AUTOEXEC.BAT file.	AUTOEXEC

The system should now be complete. Test it for each possible case, correcting errors as necessary.

Summary—Menu Systems

1. Menu systems make it easier for users to control machines.

2. New systems provide both command- and menu-driven human interfaces.

3. Menus rely on screen displays to instruct the user in their operation. Menu displays should be easy to understand, easy to use, and pleasingly formatted.

4. Developing a menu system involves:

   - Creating a text file which contains the menu and related text which will be displayed on the screen. This file is often called MENU.TXT.

   - Creating a batch file (often called MENU.BAT) to type (display) the menu text file.

   - Creating a separate batch file for each menu choice (naming each batch by the single letter or number corresponding to that menu choice). Each of these batch files contains the appropriate commands to locate and call the application program. The last line of each of these batch files contains the command MENU; this calls the file MENU.BAT, thus displaying the menu for further choices.

   - Including the command MENU as the last line of AUTOEXEC.BAT, allowing the user to turn on the computer and arrive at the menu screen automatically.

Quick Check—Menu Systems

1. What are the advantages of menu systems over command-driven systems?

2. What are the disadvantages of menu systems?

3. What is the full name of the file a user requests when he/she types "3" at the DOS prompt?

4. If MENU.BAT were not included in AUTOEXEC.BAT, how would the user request the menu?

UNIT·9·

System Management

Overview: Managing a computer system requires a few more steps, even after the logical structure of the hard disk has been created. Application programs must be installed. Often, an application program will require that certain environmental default conditions be changed to ensure the most efficient execution of the program.

In addition, managing a computer system requires the frequent backing up of files from the hard disk.

Topics: Installing Applications

Configuring Your System

Creating a CONFIG.SYS File

Configuring Your Screen with ANSI.SYS

BACKUP and RESTORE

Installing Applications

There are many possible configurations of hardware possible for DOS systems. Some factors include:

computer	IBM PC, IBM XT, IBM AT, IBM PS/2, Compaq, Zenith
display unit	IBM monochrome, composite color, RGB color
printer	parallel, serial, dot matrix, laser, brand name
modem	transmission rate, parity, brand name

Just as there are many hardware configurations, there are many applications which computer systems must perform. Some applications require special graphics, some massive data-management capabilities, and others the use of special peripheral devices.

DOS provides very general routines (called defaults) which handle most popular hardware configurations and standard applications requirements. Most of these defaults can be changed to suit the needs of particular hardware or applications. The MODE command, for example, is used to override defaults for use of the display unit, printer, or modem.

Because there are so many possible hardware configurations, programmers who write applications packages (for example, LOTUS 1-2-3, dBASE III PLUS, WordPerfect, Symphony) must design their programs to work with as many hardware configurations as possible. Many popular packages handle this problem by requiring the user to configure (setup or install) the software for their particular hardware configuration. The process of installing an application package varies by vendor and package, but may include the following steps:

- backing up the disk or copying programs to the hard disk.

- running an installation program which sets defaults in the program itself.

- creating a CONFIG.SYS file to optimize use of the program for the user's particular needs.

Configuring Your System

Creating a CONFIG.SYS File

Some application packages accept default settings for hardware during installation but allow you to expand the default limits if your needs exceed them. The dBASE III PLUS package, for example, allows the user to have fifteen files open at one time. DOS defaults to eight files open unless told to allow more. Database operations quickly exceed the limit of eight open files when indexes, report files, and so on, are considered. When DOS is booted, it looks for a file named CONFIG.SYS in the root directory of the boot disk. If the file is not found, DOS sets several default conditions and limits. To override these defaults, the user must create the appropriate CONFIG.SYS file on the disk from which DOS boots. Some of the default conditions are described below. The documentation that comes with an application package will instruct you if and how any of these defaults need to be changed. The procedure would involve creating CONFIG.SYS, if one did not already exist, or adding or modifying a line in the existing CONFIG.SYS.

BREAK=   Default=off   Option=on

Pressing CTRL SCROLL LOCK (break) interrupts programs if input or output is taking place. The CTRL SCROLL LOCK will not affect internal processes like program compilation or an infinite loop which has no input or output statement. Setting BREAK=ON will tell DOS to interrupt processing any time the CTRL SCROLL LOCK is pressed. Note that the central processing unit must do more checking for this event, and therefore will operate more slowly.

BUFFERS=   Default=2   Option=1-99

Since disk input and output is very slow compared to internal communication, DOS transfers data to or from disk a block (512 bytes) at a time. Thus, for a program which requests only 2 bytes of data DOS actually transfers 512 bytes from disk to random access memory (RAM). An area of RAM set aside by DOS for this block of data is called a buffer and requires 528 bytes. Any application which regularly uses the disk benefits from multiple buffers. The default provided by DOS is two. For applications which access large amounts of data in direct (random access) fashion, increasing the number of buffers increases the speed of processing the data, since more of it will be in RAM at any given time. The price for having many buffers is 528 bytes per buffer (which DOS reserves automatically), thus leaving less RAM for user programs and data. In general, applications requiring random access to large amounts of data (for example, database systems) work better with more buffers available.

DEVICE=   Default is the standard I/0 routines

When DOS is booted, the basic input/output system (BIOS) routines contained in read-only memory (ROM) is automatically loaded, allowing DOS to interpret key strokes correctly and form characters on the screen properly. These routines that allow the system to use physical devices are called <u>device drivers</u>. For special types of devices—for example, touch panel, special plotters, analog/digital converters—a special driver routine must be provided for DOS. Most devices come with special drivers and the user simply has to load them into memory, since they are not automatically provided in ROM. The DEVICE statement in a CONFIG.SYS file allows DOS to load these drivers. In DOS version 3.0 and above, a driver called VDISK.SYS enables the creation of an electronic, or RAM, disk. Another useful device (in this case, the device is the monitor) driver, ANSI.SYS, will be described later.

FILES=   Default=8   Option=8-255

For each file a program uses, DOS reserves some RAM (a 48-byte file control block) to keep track of that file. The number of files that DOS allows open at any time depends on how many file control blocks are available. The default number is eight, thus allowing only eight files to be used by a program. Some applications, especially database management systems, require many files to be open at once. DOS allows the user to increase the number of files at a relatively small cost in RAM space.

A CONFIG.SYS file is created by using the COPY or EDLIN commands. The file is entered and saved, but does not take effect until the next time DOS is booted from the disk containing the CONFIG.SYS file. At that time, DOS finds the file as part of its regular boot process, and sets the default values based upon its contents.

Creating a Virtual Disk

NOTE: You can create a virtual disk using DOS versions 3.0 and above. With earlier versions, you will need to purchase a program that allows the creation of a virtual disk.

What Is a Virtual Disk?

A virtual (or RAM) disk is a simulated disk drive created in a part of your computer's memory. Virtual disks have the following characteristics:

- fast access—operates at speed of computer memory.

- more than one can be installed if there is enough available RAM. They become drives D, E, F, and so on.

- disk size, sector size, and number of directory entries can all be specified for each virtual disk.

- increase resident size of DOS.

- temporary—data on a virtual disk is lost if the computer is rebooted or the power is lost.

Installing a Virtual Disk

The DOS command VDISK.SYS must be placed in the CONFIG.SYS file, thereby creating the desired disk or disks every time the computer is booted.

DEVICE=VDISK.SYS 256 128 64   Creates a 256K virtual disk having sectors of 128 bytes and allowing 64 directory entries.

Applications for a Virtual Disk

Although there are many ways to utilize a virtual disk, two of the most common applications are:

(1) for storing programs in RAM that usually would be accessed from disk, for example, all the DOS external commands, and

(2) for placing the entire application program, such as WordStar or dBASE in RAM to increase the speed of execution, or to allow subdirectories in programs which do not support them.

Configuring Your Screen and Keyboard with ANSI.SYS

ANSI.SYS is another device driver. In the same way that VDISK.SYS defines and controls a virtual disk in memory, ANSI.SYS provides more control over the keyboard and screen. It is also included in the CONFIG.SYS file using "Device= ANSI.SYS". (There may be more than one DEVICE= statement in CONFIG.SYS.)

ANSI.SYS commands can be broken down into three major types:

- Monitor foreground and background color and mode (blink, intensity)

- Cursor control

- Definition of keyboard keys

Syntax for ANSI.SYS Commands

These commands can be enacted through a batch file, by typing a text file, or through the PROMPT command. All commands begin with the {ESC} character and a left bracket {[}. How this sequence is represented depends on the way you choose to enter the command.

TEXT FILE	BATCH FILE	PROMPT
[Ctrl][V][[	ECHO [Ctrl][V][[	PROMPT $e[

What follows the initial string depends on the function of the command (see next three sections). Each command is concluded with a special character: **m** for color and mode commands, **H** for cursor position, and **p** for redefining a keyboard key. Case is important in the final character; do not use **M** for **m**.

When incorporated into a text file, the command takes effect when the file is displayed with DOS TYPE command. When incorporated into a batch file, use ECHO <ANSI.SYS command> and run the batch file. When using PROMPT, simply enter the command in addition to the characters you normally use as a prompt.

Altering the Monitor Display

The table below represents the attributes for color and mode that can be used in an ANSI.SYS command to alter the screen.

Example using PROMPT: PROMPT $e[34;46m

Example using a batch file: ECHO [Ctrl][V][[34;46m

Result: Text displays in blue on a cyan (light blue) background.

* * * * * * *

Example: PROMPT $e[3;31m

Result: Text displays blinking in red!

Notice that the three parts of the ANSI.SYS command--mode, foreground, background--are separated by semicolons.

* * * * * * *

Mode attributes:

0   All attributes off
1   High intensity (bold)
2   Underline (monochrome display only)
3   Blink
4   Reverse video
5   Invisible

Foreground Color		Background Color	
35	Black	40	Black
31	Red	41	Red
32	Green	42	Green
33	Yellow	43	Yellow
34	Blue	44	Blue
35	Magenta	45	Magenta
36	Cyan	46	Cyan
37	White	47	White

Using ANSI.SYS To Position the Cursor

Follow the initial string with the row;column position. Any text to be displayed at that location should follow immediately.

Example: PROMPT $e[12;30HWelcome to Advanced DOS

Result: The phrase will be displayed in the middle of the screen.

* * * * * * *

Redefining Keyboard Keys

Follow the initial string with the ASCII value of the key to be re-defined, followed by the ASCII value or the "character string" to be assigned to that key. The IBM extended-character set can be used in an ANSI.SYS command.

Example: PROMPT$e[96;171p   ECHO[Ctrl][V][[96;171p

Result: Defines the reverse apostrophe (‘) to be 1/2.

* * * * * * *

Example: PROMPT $e[0;32;"DIR|SORT>PRN"p

Result: Defines [Alt][D] to send a sorted directory to the printer.

Activity 9-1: Creating A CONFIG.SYS File

The following CONFIG.SYS file is appropriate for use with dBase III PLUS and most other current applications. If two programs you are installing have conflicting values for a default, use the greater of the two. For example, if one program requires the statement FILES=20, and another program requires FILES=15, use FILES=20 in your CONFIG.SYS.

CONFIG.SYS must be stored in the root directory; changes made to it have no effect, unless the system is re-booted. CONFIG.SYS is loaded into RAM before AUTOEXEC.BAT. Therefore, no PATH statement is in effect for files used in CONFIG.SYS. If a device driver file is included, the full path address for that file must be given.

Task	Procedure
Make sure the root directory of A: is the default.	A:
Use the COPY command to enter the three lines of text. **NOTE:** Be sure to include the full path to ANSI.SYS.	COPY CON CONFIG.SYS BREAK=ON FILES=20 BUFFERS=24 DEVICE=C:\DOS\ANSI.SYS
Exit the COPY command data entry mode.	[F6] [Return]
Check to see whether the file appears in the directory.	DIR
Examine the contents of the file.	TYPE CONFIG.SYS
Since CONFIG.SYS is loaded only when the system boots, reboot.	[Ctrl][Alt][Del]
Exit the automatically loaded menu system.	4 [Return]

Activity 9-2: Using ANSI.SYS Commands

This activity is appropriate only for use with a color monitor. Screen colors can be customized by using ANSI.SYS commands in conjunction with the PROMPT command.

Task	Procedure
Add an ANSI.SYS command to your default prompt to generate white characters on a blue background.	PROMPT $e[37;44m$P$G
See the full screen in its new colors.	CLS
Experiment with other color combinations (refer to codes in section on <u>Altering the Monitor Display</u> in Unit IX to find the one you like best).	

Backing Up a Hard Disk: BACKUP and RESTORE

Backing up data is critical for all serious computer operations. When using a hard disk, you will need many floppy disks (or a streaming tape backup unit) to regularly backup your data or programs. DOS provides two utilities for backing up and restoring data: BACKUP and RESTORE.

BACKUP can be used to backup selected files or the entire hard disk. The system will prompt you to put floppy disks in the A: drive as needed. Label these floppy disks "Backup 1," "Backup 2," and so on, because they must be restored in the same order. All floppy disks must be formatted but should not have the system on them. The files being backed up are called source files and the resulting copies are called backup files.

There are four options which may be added to the BACKUP command.

/A (Add) Source files will be added to any existing files on the backup disk. If you do not specify the /A, any files on the floppy disks will be erased! You cannot use /A for the initial backup.

/M (Modified) Only backs up those files which have been changed since the last backup.

/S (Subdirectories) Backs up all files in all subdirectories of the specified (or default) directory.

/D (Date) Allows the user to specify a date, thus directing DOS to only backup files dated after it.

Backup files are not functional files, since they contain control data which the RESTORE command needs to restore them to the hard disk. Use the COPY command if you want a functional copy of files on a hard disk. You must use the RESTORE command to restore the backup files to the hard disk and return them to an operational state. The RESTORE command will prompt you to insert your backup disks in the proper order in drive A:.

Once your system is set up—all your directories are made and your programs are installed—it is recommended that you BACKUP the entire hard disk. If your hard disk should crash (fail), you can restore the original structure. For making backup copies of <u>data</u> files, it is usually recommended to use the COPY command to duplicate files from the hard disk onto a floppy. In this way, your data files are still useable even if your hard disk fails.

Activity 9-3: Backing Up Selected Files From the Hard Disk to A Floppy Disk

Note: If you are using DOS 2.1 or an earlier version, you must have a hard disk system to complete this activity. Versions 3.0 and later will allow the BACKUP command to be used to back up files from one floppy to another, between floppy and hard disk, and between hard disks.

Task	Procedure/Response
Place a blank formatted disk in drive A:.	
Change the default drive to C:.	C:
Change the current directory to the one where DOS external commands are stored.	CD\DOS
Backup all the files from the DOS directory which have an .EXE extension.	BACKUP C:\DOS*.EXE A:
Make A: the default drive.	A:
When the files have been copied, check your directory.	DIR
What file did BACKUP create?	_____
Attempt to use the file SORT.EXE.	DIR|SORT

NOTE: BACKUP files must be RESTOREd to be useable.

On Your Own—System Management

Task	Procedure/Response
Edit your AUTOEXEC.BAT file to incorporate color into your prompt.	_____
Add the command to allow the full screen to show the new colors.	_____
Reboot your completely configured system.	_____

Summary—System Management

1. Hardware configurations and software packages must be compatible. Most software vendors provide a procedure for making their package compatible with your hardware. Run the installation procedure carefully.

2. Once an application program is installed on a hard disk for the appropriate equipment, the user can further configure, or customize, the program to particular needs. These "set-up" programs are usually menu driven, and allow changes to program defaults.

3. A CONFIG.SYS file is sought each time DOS boots. If it is not found, DOS sets many defaults. A CONFIG.SYS file can be created using COPY CON or EDLIN. It may contain commands to increase the number of files allowed to be open at one time, and the number of buffers. Increasing the number of buffers, within reason, tends to speed up certain disk-based operations.

4. CONFIG.SYS can also contain device drivers which give the user expanded control over such devices as the monitor, the keyboard, mice, printers, and so on. One such device driver for the monitor and keyboard is ANSI.SYS, a DOS external program.

5. Using ANSI.SYS commands with the PROMPT command allows the user to customize monitor colors.

6. The BACKUP command is used to make copies of individual files, complete subdirectories, or an entire hard disk onto floppies. The RESTORE command returns those backed up files to the hard disk.

Quick Check—System Management

1. What are some reasons that application software must be installed?

2. What happens if there is no CONFIG.SYS file on disk?

3. How would you use ANSI.SYS commands and the PROMPT command to customize your prompt to show the current path and the greater-than symbol as black characters on a red background?

4. What are the differences between the following commands:

   COPY C:*.* A: and   BACKUP C:*.* A:

Appendix A—Activities from Unit III for Dual Floppy Systems

This section, for computer systems having dual floppy drives and no hard disk, replaces corresponding pages in UNIT III.

Activity 3.1: Getting Started

Task	Procedure/Response
Place your DOS disk in drive A:. Place your student disk in drive B:.	
Power up (boot) the system: Wait for a POST.	Turn on the computer and monitor.
NOTE: On some computers you will see numbers incrementing at the top of your screen. This is the part of POST called the RAM check—checking all the memory chips.	
NOTE: After the POST, DOS is automatically loaded into RAM.	
A <u>default</u> condition is an assumption—what is assumed unless you specifically indicate an alternate condition. Defaults can almost always be changed.	
Notice the default (assumed) date. Is it correct?	_____
What is the format in which the date is displayed?	_____
Enter the date in the proper format.	mm-dd-yy[Return]
Notice the default time. Is it correct?	_____

| **Task** | **Procedure/Response** |

What is the format in which the time is displayed?   _____

Enter the date in the proper format.   hh:mm[Return]

What do you see on the screen?   _____

The letter A, and the greater-than symbol, (>) are the default DOS <u>prompt</u>. This is the drive from which DOS was loaded and to which any command or request will be directed.

The small blinking underline is the <u>cursor</u>. It marks the position where typed characters will appear on the screen.

Activity 3-2: DOS Housekeeping Commands

DOS has a number of commands that can be used to give the operator additional information and control. If you have booted your computer and bypassed the date and time, you can enter or edit them from the DOS prompt. DOS commands can be entered in upper- or lowercase letters.

Task	Procedure/Response
REMINDER: Always press [Return] when you finish typing a command. This is DOS's signal to execute the command.	
Verify the date.	DATE
Accept the new default.	[Return]
Verify the time.	TIME
Accept the new default.	[Return]
NOTE: DOS uses a 24-hour clock. If it is 1:00 pm, enter 13:00.	
Clear all this data from the screen.	CLS
Determine the version of DOS you are using.	VER
What version is it?	_____
Determine whether this disk has a label.	VOL
What is the volume label?	_____
Determine whether your student disk has a label.	VOL B:

Task	Procedure/Response

NOTE: DOS assumed you wanted the label of the disk in the default drive when you just entered VOL. You must override that assumption if you want the label of the disk in drive B:.

Name your student disk (DOS 3.0 and greater only).   LABEL B:

If you had just typed LABEL, what disk would you be naming?   _____

You may use up to eleven characters, including spaces. Upper- or lowercase is acceptable.

What volume label did you give your disk?   _____

Confirm your new volume label.   LABEL B:

What message is displayed?   _____

Respond to the message, but do not delete your label.   [Return] N

Appendix A **181**

Activity 3-3: Displaying A Disk's Contents: DIR   CHKDSK

The files stored on a disk are listed in the directory. The DIR command not only displays the names of the files but their size, date, and time of creation. In addition, DIR lists the amount of available space on your disk. The CHKDSK command gives information about disk space in addition to the amount of total and available memory. The initial <u>default disk drive</u> is the disk from which DOS was loaded into RAM.

You must press the [Return] or [Enter] key to activate a DOS command.

<u>Task</u>	<u>Procedure/Response</u>
Clear the screen.	CLS
Display the directory of the default disk.	DIR
You are viewing the contents of which disk?	_____
Stop/start the directory from scrolling.	DIR [Ctrl][S]
View the directory in screens.	DIR/P
Display a wide directory.	DIR/W
Look for a specific file.	DIR COMMAND.COM
Display the directory of your student disk.	DIR B:
How many files are named in this directory?	_____
What is the volume label?	_____
Look for a specific file on your student disk.	DIR B:READ.ME
If you did not include B:, on which disk would DOS look for the READ.ME file?	_____

Task	Procedure/Response
How does the directory listing separate a file name from its extension?	_____
What must you type to separate a file name from its extension?	_____
Display a group of files.	DIR B:*.COM DIR B:*.TXT
Where are these files?	_____
What is the default drive?	_____
How many .TXT files are there?	_____
Change the default to the B: drive.	B:
How has the DOS prompt changed?	_____
View the default directory.	DIR
Which disk's directory are you viewing?	_____
How would you now request a directory of drive A:?	_____
View all the .EXE files on the default drive.	DIR *.EXE
How does DOS respond if there are no files with the name you requested?	_____
Check the disk and memory status.	CHKDSK
What disk are you checking?	_____
Check the boot disk.	CHKDSK A:

On Your Own

Write the complete command you would use to accomplish the tasks. Execute the command to answer the questions.

Task	Procedure	Response
What day of the week will July 4, 1990, be?	_____	_____
Return the default date to today.	_____	
How many bytes does COMMAND.COM occupy on drive A:?	_____	_____
What time was MEMO.TXT stored on your student disk?	_____	_____
How much space is left on your student disk?	_____	_____
How many hidden files are on your student disk?	_____	_____
Delete the volume label from your student disk.	_____	
How many hidden files are there now?	_____	_____
What did the hidden file contain?	_____	
Restore your volume label.	_____	

The COPY Command

The DOS COPY command is a powerful and flexible program for transferring files between disks, between system devices, and for backing up files to the same disk. It can also be used to create files and to merge several files into one. COPY does not affect the original file, but simply makes an exact copy. The COMP (Compare) command is used to verify the accuracy of the copy when very important data is being transferred. COPY does not indicate that a file of the same name exists on the target disk; therefore, it is possible to write over a file by accident.

When using COPY the following rules apply:

- The <u>source</u> disk is the disk you are copying FROM.

- The <u>target</u> disk is the disk you are copying TO.

- If no drive is specified for the source or for the target drive, COPY copies from and to the current (default) drive.

- If you are backing up a file to the same disk, you must change the name of the file or the file extension, since two files with identical names cannot exist on the same disk.

    Example: A>COPY MEMO OLDMEMO
               A>COPY MEMO MEMO.BAK

- If a file has an extension, that extension must be used in the COPY command; otherwise you will get the "File not found" error message.

- Spaces are used in COPY to separate the source file from the target file. As with all DOS commands, do not use a space between the drive designator and the file name.

    Example: A>COPY B:MEMO A:OLDMEMO

    In this example, you would not be required to include the A: designator since the default drive is A; however, using drive designators clarifies exactly what is happening in the COPY procedure.

- If you simply want to rename a file and not produce a second copy, use the RENAME command, that is, RENAME MEMO OLDMEMO. After this command, the file MEMO will no longer exist.

Appendix A **185**

Activity 3-4: Copying and Verifying Files: COPY COMP

Task	Procedure/Response
Make sure drive B: is the default.	B:
View the contents of the student disk.	DIR
Copy MEMO.TXT to OLDMEMO.	COPY MEMO.TXT OLDMEMO
Does MEMO.TXT still exist?	_____
Make sure.	DIR MEMO.TXT
What message indicates a successful copy?	_____
Create a backup for NOTICE.	COPY NOTICE NOTICE.BAK
Verify your work.	DIR
To which disk were the two new files copied?	_____
How many files are now on your student disk?	_____
Copy all the files with the .TXT extension from the student disk to the boot disk.	COPY *.TXT A:
What disk is the assumed source?	_____
What response does DOS give when it copies a group of files?	_____
Check the copy with COMP.	COMP B:*.TXT A:*.TXT
What message does DOS display if files are identical?	_____
Confirm that all the .TXT files are now also on A:	DIR A:*.TXT

Task	Procedure/Response
Create backups for all the files with a .TXT extension.	COPY A:*.TXT A:*.BAK
If you did not type the second A:, where would the .BAK files be?	_____
Confirm that all the .BAK files were created.	DIR A:*.BAK
What first names do these files have?	_____
Rename OLDMEMO to NEWMEMO.	RENAME OLDMEMO NEWMEMO
What drive is assumed?	_____
Verify your work.	DIR

DISKCOPY and DISKCOMP

Two DOS external commands, DISKCOPY and DISKCOMP, allow you to copy the contents of an entire floppy disk (including directories if they have been made on the floppy) and then verify that the two disks are exactly alike. The DISKCOPY program formats the target disk as it copies files. Although this seems like a simpler procedure than COPY, it is used far less frequently for the following reasons:

- Since DISKCOPY formats the target disk, it is very easy to erase valuable files when you really want to add the files on the source disk to the target disk.

- Files cannot be copied to or from a fixed disk using DISKCOPY: an error message will result if this is attempted.

- Because the target disk is formatted, the version of DOS on the source disk will be transferred, which may not be what you desire.

- If the source disk has undergone a great deal of file creation and deletion, the diskette space will be fragmented, causing delays in reading and writing on the target disk. The recommended procedure in copying these disks is to use COPY *.*, which will compress the files when they are written to the target disk.

DISKCOPY is an acceptable procedure for backing up floppy data disks for archival purposes. It is mandatory for copying directory structure; COPY *.* copies only files in the current directory. DISKCOMP is used following a DISKCOPY to verify the accuracy of the new disk.

Activity 3-5: Deleting Files: DEL ERASE

Two identical commands exist for removing files from a disk, DEL and ERASE. Both can be used to delete single files and groups of files using global and wildcard characters. Special programs like Norton Utilities can recover files that have been accidentally erased, if nothing else has been written to the disk in that space. This is possible since DEL or ERASE simply deletes the file entry from the directory so that it can no longer be accessed; it does not physically erase the contents of the file from the disk. The space that the file occupied is marked as available, however; and if another file is saved over it, there is no way it can be recovered.

To erase the entire contents of a disk for reuse, use the ERASE command with global characters, ERASE *.*. You will be prompted with the following message: "Are you sure (Y/N)?" to which you must respond. This is a failsafe device, since this command will wipe out your entire disk. USE IT CAREFULLY.

Task	Procedure/Response
Erase the file NEWMEMO.	ERASE NEWMEMO
From what disk was this file erased?	_____
Delete the .TXT files copied in the previous activity.	DEL A:*.TXT
What message indicates a group of files has been deleted?	_____
Delete the .BAK files from the boot disk.	DEL A:*.BAK
Check the directory to verify the results.	DIR A:

Activity 3-6: Viewing the Contents of A File: TYPE

Text files created under DOS can be viewed on the screen or sent to the printer using the TYPE command. Files created in most word-processing programs can also be viewed using TYPE but will be difficult to read, since all formatting is lost and format characters display as extraneous symbols. The .COM and .EXE files cannot be viewed in this manner, as they are not stored in "human-readable" form.

An important application of TYPE is in viewing the contents of a READ.ME file. These files are often put on purchased software to indicate updates and changes in the program that have not been included in the documentation. Always check a new program for a READ.ME file, since they generally contain valuable information.

Task	Procedure/Response
View the contents of your disk's MEMO.TXT file.	TYPE MEMO.TXT
Can you clearly read all the words?	_____
View the contents of the file named NOTICE.	TYPE NOTICE
Was NOTICE stored in a DOS-readable format?	_____
Try to view the contents of COMMAND.COM.	TYPE A:COMMAND.COM
Why can't you understand the contents?	_____
View the contents of SDIR.DOC.	TYPE SDIR.DOC
Control the scrolling.	[Ctrl][S]
Read the READ.ME file. Cancel the scrolling.	TYPE READ.ME [Ctrl][C]
Are SDIR.DOC and READ.ME DOS-readable files?	_____

Redirecting Input and Output

The standard output device is the screen or monitor. That is, the output of all commands are generally sent to the screen for viewing. The standard input device is the keyboard. DOS allows both input and output to be redirected to other than the standard devices. A file can receive the results of a command. This file could then be used with a word processing application, for example, to become part of a larger manuscript. The printer can also be an output device, with results of commands redirected to it to allow for hardcopy output.

The following symbols redirect input/output:

>**PRN**   causes output of command to be directed to the printer (PRN) rather than to the monitor

>**[filename]** causes file to be created and output to be directed to this file

>>**[filename]** causes file to be opened and output directed to end of file

<**[filename]** causes input to come from file as opposed to keyboard

Activity 3-7: Redirecting Output

Task	Procedure/Response
*** Turn on your printer before continuing ***	
Send a copy of the directory of your student disk to the printer.	DIR>PRN
Store a copy of the directory in a file.	DIR>DIR.FIL
On what disk has this file been created?	_____
NOTE: This file could be read by any word-processing program; it could be edited to provide an annotated directory list.	
How could you view the contents of this new file?	_____
Get hard copy (printed copy) of the results of the CHKDSK command.	CHKDSK>PRN
Print a copy of the file SDIR.DOC.	TYPE SDIR.DOC>PRN

Using Pipes and Filters

Piping allows the standard output of one program to be used as the standard input to another program. Temporary files are created in the root directory to hold the data being piped. The pipe symbol is the broken vertical line above the backslash on the lower left side of the keyboard. In this manual it will appear as a solid line (|).

A filter is a program or command that reads data from a standard input device, modifies the data, then writes the result to a standard output device. The three standard DOS filters are:

MORE — breaks output (typically from the TYPE command) into screen-sized units for display

SORT — sorts data alphabetically

FIND — searches output for a specific string of characters and displays only those lines which contain that string

By combining redirection, pipes, and filters, the output of one program, for example, TYPE, is piped (|) to the filter program which performs an action on it and delivers the result to the screen, printer, or another file as directed. These filters can also be used as stand-alone commands.

Appendix A 193

Activity 3-8: Variations on TYPE: Pipes and Filters

Task	Procedure/Response
View the contents of the READ.ME file.	TYPE READ.ME
View the contents of this file one screen at a time.	TYPE READ.ME|MORE
What message indicates that you should continue?	_____
How can you continue?	_____
Find a specific character string in the SDIR.DOC file.	TYPE SDIR.DOC|FIND "sort"
Are only lines containing the distinct word "sort" found?	_____
How many lines in SDIR.DOC contain the characters "sort"?	_____
Find a specific character string in the MEMO.TXT file.	TYPE MEMO.TXT|FIND "EDLIN"
Try to find lines of output that contain the characters "Edlin".	TYPE MEMO.TXT|FIND "Edlin"
Is case significant to the FIND filter?	_____
Print the lines that contain "EDLIN".	TYPE MEMO.TXT|FIND "EDLIN">PRN
Display the contents of WORDS.TXT.	TYPE WORDS.TXT
Sort the file alphabetically by first character of each line.	TYPE WORDS.TXT|SORT

Task	Procedure/Response
Redirect the output of the above command to a file.	TYPE WORDS.TXT|SORT>WORDSORT.TXT
View the contents of the new file.	TYPE WORDSORT.TXT
How could you print the contents?	_____
Has WORDS.TXT been changed?	_____
Verify your answer.	TYPE WORDS.TXT
See the directory entry for the new file.	DIR *.TXT
When was it created?	_____
Send an alphabetically sorted directory to the printer.	DIR|SORT>PRN

NOTE: The first two numbered files are temporary files created by the SORT filter.

Send a directory sorted in descending order (reverse).	DIR|SORT/R>PRN
Sort the directory by file size.	DIR|SORT/+16

NOTE: This version of SORT rearranges each line of output according to the 16th character on each line. In some lines, the 16th character is blank or a character other than a number.

On Your Own—DOS Basics

Task	Procedure	Response
Turn off the computer if it is on.		
Boot up.	_____	
Respond to DATE and TIME prompts.	_____	
Print a directory of the default drive.	_____	
Change the default drive to the one containing your student disk.	_____	
Print out the text of WORDSORT.TXT.	_____	
Change the name of WORDSORT.TXT to SORTLIST.	_____	
Must all DOS-readable files have a .TXT extension?		_____
Does renaming a file change its date?	_____	_____
Copy COMMAND.COM from the boot disk to your student disk.	_____	
Does copying a file change its date?	_____	_____
Make the boot disk the default.	_____	
View an alphabetical listing of the default directory.	_____	
If two files have the same first name, which one does SORT alphabetize first?		_____
What comes first in SORTed order, numbers or letters?		_____
Are spaces alphabetized before or after numbers?		_____

196 The DOS Book

| **Task** | **Procedure** | **Response** |

Choose a file on your student disk and make a backup copy of it on the same disk.

APPENDIX B—Activity from UNIT IV for Dual Floppy Systems

This activity for computer systems with dual floppy drives and no hard disk replaces the corresponding activity in UNIT IV.

Activity 4-3: Checking Disk Validity

Task	Procedure/Response
Be sure the default drive contains your student disk.	B:
At the prompt, tell the computer to check the disk.	CHKDSK
The program may tell you it has found lost clusters. If so, it will ask: CONVERT LOST CHAINS TO FILES (Y/N)?	Y
If there were lost clusters, take a look at them:	DIR *.CHK
Display a listing of all the file names.	CHKDSK/V
Which is the hidden file?	_____
What do you think it contains?	_____
Check the integrity of all the files in the directory.	CHKDSK *.*
If a file is reported noncontiguous, copy it to a file with a different name. CHKDSK that file. It should now be contiguous. Delete the original file and rename the new file with the original name.	
Check the boot disk.	CHKDSK A:

Task

Display a listing of all the files on the boot disk.

Be prepared to suspend the scrolling.

What are the names of the two hidden boot files near the beginning of the list?

Procedure/Response

CHKDSK C:/V

[Ctrl][S]

_____

Appendix C—Answers to Quick Checks and On Your Own

Answers to Quick Checks

UNIT I: Introduction to Microcomputer Hardware and Software

1. b,d,e
2. c
3. d
4. a
5. a,b,d,e

UNIT II: Identifying the Role of Personal Computers in the Workplace

1. c
2. g
3. d
4. c
5. e
6. b
7. a
8. g (c)
9. e
10. d
11. f

UNIT III: DOS Basics

1. A disk's directory can be printed by redirecting the output of the DIR command to the printer: DIR>PRN. It can also be printed by displaying the directory listing on the screen, then printing the screen with [Shift][PrtSc].

2. Global filenames are used when an action is to be performed on a group of files all having part of their name in common. For example, COPYing a group of files with the same extension; ERASEing a group of files with the same first three letters in their names.

3. Directories can be viewed with DIR/P (one screen page at a time) or with DIR/W (wide).

4. Internal commands are part of COMMAND.COM and are always present in RAM. External commands are files, with .COM or .EXE extensions, that are stored on disk and must be loaded each time they are to be used.

5. ERASE *.* erases all the files from the current directory.

6. The letter in the prompt identifies the default drive.

UNIT IV: Additional External Commands

1. External commands are loaded into RAM from disk when their names are typed at the DOS prompt.

2. The PRINT command allows DOS-readable files to be printed while the computer is being used for other tasks. It can print files created by word processors if those files were stored in DOS-readable, or ASCII, format. Special word processing formatting effects such as boldfacing or underlining will not be printed.

3. ATTRIB +R does not prevent a file from being copied; it prevents the original file from being changed or deleted. The read-only attribute is not copied to the new file.

4. A long directory could be printed on an IBM graphics-compatible computer by changing the printer's default mode to 132 characters per inch and eight lines per inch.

    MODE LPT1:132,8

UNIT V: Disk Organization

1. b
2. d
3. a
4. b
5. c
6. d
7. a
8. c
9. a,b,c
10. d

UNIT VI: Creating DOS Files

1. The file FILE8.MY can be created with the command

    COPY CON FILE8.MY

2. A line editor permits editing a single line at a time. Only the current line is available for changing. A screen editor allows access to any line on the screen using the up- and down-arrow keys.

3. The [F6] key (or typing [Ctrl][Z] — ^Z) marks the end of the source file when using COPY CON.

4. COPY is an internal command and thus is always available to create a short file. It is faster than EDLIN. The disadvantage to using COPY rather than EDLIN is that COPY does not allow editing of a line once it has been entered. To change a previous line, the entire file must be recreated.

UNIT VII: Batch Files

1. a,b,c,d
2. b,c
3. b
4. a,b,c
5. a,c
6. b
7. b,d
8. a,c,d
9. b
10. a,b

UNIT VIII: Creating a Menu System

1. Menu-driven systems enable users unfamiliar with the operating system to load applications and do other pre-defined operations.

2. Menu systems have the disadvantages of being inflexible—only operations which have been incorporated into the menu can be performed. They are also slower and more cumbersome than initiating the same command sequences at the DOS prompt.

3. When a user types 3, the batch file 3.BAT is being loaded.

4. A user could request the menu by entering at the DOS prompt the first name of the menu batch file—MENU.

UNIT IX: System Management

1. Application software must be installed to make the most efficient use of the hardware available.

2. If there is no CONFIG.SYS file, DOS sets many system defaults.

3. A prompt showing the current path and the greater-than (>) symbol as black characters on a red background would be created with the command

    PROMPT $e[30;41m$P$G

4. COPY C:*.* A: makes duplicate copies on the disk in drive A: of all the files in the root directory of drive C:. The files on A: can be loaded and used from that disk.

    BACKUP C:*.* A: makes backup copies on the disk in drive A: of all the files in the root directory of drive C:. The files on A: can only be loaded and used after being RESTOREd to drive C:. They are not useable from the floppy.

Solutions to On Your Own

On Your Own—DOS Basics

Write the complete command you would use to accomplish the tasks. Execute the command to answer the questions.

Task	Procedure	Response
What day of the week will July 4, 1990, be?	DATE [Return] 7/4/88 [Return] DATE [Return]	Wednesday
Return the default date to today.	DATE [Return] <today's date> [Return]	
How many bytes does COMMAND.COM occupy on drive C:?	DIR C:COMMAND.COM	23210 (Ver. 3.1)
What time was MEMO.TXT stored on your student disk?	DIR A:MEMO.TXT	12.05 pm
How much space is left on your student disk?	DIR A:	339968 bytes
How many hidden files are on your student disk?	CHKDSK A:	1
Delete the volume label from your student disk.	LABEL A: [Return] [Return] Y	
How many hidden files are there now?	CHKDSK A:	0
What did the hidden file contain?		Volume label
Restore your volume label.	LABEL A: [Return] <your label> [Return]	

Task	Procedure	Response
Turn off the computer if it is on.		
Boot up.	Turn on CPU and monitor	
Respond to DATE and TIME prompts.	\<today's date\> [Return] \<current time\> [Return]	
Print a directory of the default drive.	DIR>PRN	
Change the default drive to the one containing your student disk.	A:	
Print out the text of WORDSORT.TXT.	TYPE WORDSORT.TXT> PRN	
Change the name of WORDSORT.TXT to SORTLIST.	RENAME WORDSORT.TXT SORTLIST	
Must all DOS-readable files have a .TXT extension?		NO
Does renaming a file change its date?	DIR	NO
Copy COMMAND.COM from the hard disk to your student disk.	COPY C:COMMAND.COM	
Does copying a file change its date?	DIR C:COMMAND.COM DIR COMMAND.COM	NO
Make the boot disk the default.	C:	

Task	Procedure	Response
View an alphabetical listing of the default directory.	DIR|SORT	
If two files have the same first name, which one does SORT alphabetize first?		The one with the alphabetically first extension.
What comes first in SORTed order, numbers or letters?		Numbers
Are spaces alphabetized before or after numbers?		Before
Choose a file on your student disk and make a backup copy of it on the same disk.	COPY MEMO.TXT MEMO.BAK (or any other file)	

On Your Own—Additional External Commands

Task	Procedure	Response
Be sure the student disk is the default.		A:
Display the directory of your student disk on a 40-character screen.	MODE 40 DIR	
Change the MODE back to 80 if you prefer, or leave it at 40.	MODE 80	
Determine the total amount of RAM your computer has.	CHKDSK	655360 (640K)
How much is used by the operating system?	655360-609912	45448 (Ver 3.1)
Using two different commands, determine the amount of space remaining on your student disk.	CHKDSK DIR	336896 336896
Do the two numbers agree?		YES
Protect all the .DOC files on your student disk from accidental erasure.	ATTRIB +R *.DOC	
View the attributes of all the files on your student disk.	ATTRIB *.*	
How many files are read-only?		2

Task	Procedure	Response

Suppose you had tried to TYPE the READ.ME file and had seen a lot of extraneous "garbage" characters on the screen. The file seemed to be shorter than it should be. How would you try to fix it?

    RECOVER READ.ME

How many bytes recover successfully?

                          3565

Challenge:

Print the names of all the .COM files on your boot disk, including the hidden files.

    CHKDSK C:/V|FIND ".COM">PRN

The three .COM files on your student disk are utility programs which are not part of DOS but which use and expand upon DOS commands. Read the documentation that comes with two of them. They are loaded just like DOS external commands (by typing their name). Experiment with all three. Which DOS command does each enhance? Read the screen for additional information while these programs are executing.

                        FREE enhances DIR
                        SDIR enhances DIR|SORT
                        LIST enhances TYPE

On Your Own—Disk Organization

Task	Procedure/Response
Use your own name to make a personal directory which is a subdirectory of the root of A:.	CD \ MD <name>
Change into your own directory.	CD \ <name>
What is your prompt?	A:\><name>
Copy NOTICE and MEMO1.TXT from your \Word\Letters subdirectory into your own directory.	COPY \WORD\LETTERS\NOTICE COPY \WORD\LETTERS\MEMO1.TXT
Remove NOTICE and MEMO1.TXT from the \Word\Letters subdirectory.	ERASE \WORD\LETTERS\NOTICE DEL \WORD\LETTERS\MEMO1.TXT or CD\WORD\LETTERS ERASE NOTICE DEL MEMO1.TXT
Create a two-line prompt that shows the current Time on the first line and the current path and greater-than symbol on the second.	PROMPT T_ PG
Return to the root directory.	CD \
What is your prompt?	<TIME> A:\>
Print a TREE of all the directories and all the files on your student disk.	TREE/F>PRN

On Your Own—Creating DOS Files

Task	Procedure/Response
Use the SUBST command to make it easier to indicate the location of MYNOTE. Create the new drive F:.	SUBST F: \WORD\MEMOS\SMITH
View a directory of your new drive.	DIR F:
How many files does it contain?	3
EDLIN MYNOTE (remember to tell DOS where to find MYNOTE). Add a few more lines. Print the new version.	EDLIN F:MYNOTE L 6i (or number following last line) [Ctrl][C] L E TYPE F:MYNOTE>PRN
Create a short note with COPY CON (call it MYNOTE2) in the root directory. Tell a friend of your plans for the weekend.	COPY CON \MYNOTE2 <your text> [Return] <your text> [Return] [F6] [Return]
Print MYNOTE2.	TYPE \MYNOTE2>PRN

Challenge:

Task	Procedure/Response
Use the computer as a typewriter. Create a letter to your grandmother (or someone else) that is created at the console and printed but never saved in a file.	COPY CON PRN
What is the source?	CON
What is the destination?	PRN

On Your Own—Batch Files

Task	Procedure/Response
Change to your \BATCH directory.	CD \BATCH
Create a batch file called D that will display a directory of the disk in drive A:.	COPY CON D.BAT DIR A: [F6]
What extension must your file have?	.BAT
Modify D.BAT so DOS commands are not ECHOed to the screen and the directory displays on a clear screen.	EDLIN D.BAT 1I ECHO OFF CLS [Ctrl][C] E
Modify D.BAT so it can be used to display a directory of any disk the user requests.	EDLIN D.BAT 3 DIR %1 E
Use D.BAT to see a directory of the hard disk.	D C:
Modify your AUTOEXEC.BAT to insert three blank lines between the message "Welcome Back" and the message produced by PAUSE.	EDLIN \AUTOEXEC.BAT 9I [Alt]255 [Alt]255 [Alt]255 [Ctrl][C] E

On Your Own—System Management

<u>Task</u>

Edit your AUTOEXEC.BAT file to incorporate color into your prompt.

Add the command to allow the full screen to show the new colors.

Reboot your completely configured system.

<u>Procedure/Response</u>

EDLIN \AUTOEXEC.BAT
7
[F]$[Return]
[Ins]$e[37;44m[F3]

       or

7
PROMPT $e[37;44m$p$g

8I
CLS
[Ctrl][C]
L
E

[Ctrl][Alt][Del]

Index

ANSI.SYS, 161
ASSIGN, 71, 78
ATTRIB, 65
AUTOEXEC.BAT, 123, 137

BACKUP, 88
Batch Files, 123; commands, 123; comparison of batch files and text files, 125; names, 124; variables, 131

CD, 88, 89
CHKDSK, 34
CHKDSK/V, 88
CHKDSK/F, 67
CLS, 39
Command vs. Menu-Driven Systems, 145
Communications, 21
Computer Software, 8; rules for floppy disk care, 9
Computer Hardware, 2; CPU, 2; Input/Output Devices, 3
CONFIG.SYS, 161; creating a CONFIG.SYS file, 163-64
COPY, CON 112, 118
COPY, 33, 57; command, 44

Database Management Systems, 16, 24
DATE, command option, 34; internal command, 33
DEL, 33
Desktop Publishing, 16, 24
DIR, 88, 108; command option, 34; internal command, 33
DISKCOMP, 47
DISKCOPY, 47; external command, 34
DOS, 8-41; controlling DOS from the keyboard, 35; commands, 33; external, 34; internal, 33; file and disk management, 30; housekeeping, 39; options, 34; filenames, 27, 32; global filename characters, 32

EDLIN, 114, 115
ERASE, internal command, 33

FDISK, 86
FIND, 58
FORMAT, 83; external command, 34
Formatting Disks, 83

Graphics, 21, 24

Hard Disk Organization, 85; Logical Organization, 86; Physical Organization, 84

Installing Applications, 162

LABEL, 40
LABEL, 41; external command, 34

Mapping a Directory Structure, 148
MD, 88, 108
Memory, 3; RAM, 3; ROM, 3
Menu design, 143; characteristics, 146; creation, 147; menu driven system, 145; MENU.BAT file, 148; MENU.TXT, 148
Microfloppies, 9
MODE, 72
MORE, 54
MS-DOS and PC-DOS, 27

Networking, 23, 24

Operating Systems, 27, 28; DOS, 8; OS/2, 9

PATH, 89; command, 104, 105; internal command, 88
PRINT, 62, 78; external command, 34
PROMPT, 108; command, 96; moving between directories, 89

RD, 88, 108

RECOVER, 78
Redirecting Input and Output, 27, 50
RENAME, 58; internal command, 33; within copy command, 44
RESTORE, 108; external, 88

SORT, 54
Spreadsheets, 13, 19
Subdirectories, 108; file specification, 100; guidelines, 87-88
SUBST, 106

TIME, 33
TREE/F, 88
TREE, 81, 108; external command, 88; structured directory, 86
TYPE, 33; pipes and filters, 52

VER, 39
Virtual, Disk 165
VOL, 39

Wildcards, 32
Word Processing 14, 24; desktop publishing, 16